D0311073

German
Grammar

WILLIAM ROWLINSON

Oxford   New York
OXFORD UNIVERSITY PRESS
1993

Oxford University Press, Walton Street, Oxford OX2 6DP

*Oxford New York Toronto
Delhi Bombay Calcutta Madras Karachi
Kuala Lumpur Singapore Hong Kong Tokyo
Nairobi Dar es Salaam Cape Town
Melbourne Auckland Madrid*

*and associated companies in
Berlin Ibadan*

Oxford is a trade mark of Oxford University Press

British Library Cataloguing in Publication Data

Data available

Library of Congress Cataloging in Publication Data

*Rowlinson, W.
German grammar/William Rowlinson.
p. cm.—(Oxford minireference) Includes index.
1. German language—Grammar—1950– 2. German language—
Textbooks for foreign speakers—English. I. Title. II. Series
438.2'421—dc20 PF3112.R67 1993 92–38572*

ISBN 0-19-211677-0

*Typeset by Pentacor PLC, High Wycombe, Bucks
Printed in Great Britain by
Charles Letts (Scotland) Ltd.
Dalkeith, Scotland*

I Introduction

This German Grammar is small enough to slip into any pocket or handbag, but is more thorough, more accurate, and more practical than other pocket grammars. It is also more up to date. In the next 300 pages you will find:

■ All the basic grammar of German presented clearly, comprehensively, and succinctly.

■ Explanations that use everyday language, and a glossary of absolutely all the grammatical terms we have used.

■ Up-to-date explanations of modern German usage not found in other grammars of this size.

■ Short, simple, easy-to-follow German examples for points of basic grammar, and longer examples from modern German sources where they are needed to explain usage.

■ A clear layout within a tough binding that will stand up to hard use.

This grammar is *really* comprehensive. It will explain problems met by beginners, it will be a reliable learning aid for GCSE and A level, and it will remain a first resource for quick reference and revision for German specialists who have reached university and polytechnic level. As well as covering all the grammar used in modern German, with particular stress on the difference between the spoken and the written language, it has sections on translation problems, word order, and punctuation, and verb tables with the conjugation of all the irregular verbs used in modern German. A feature of this grammar is its comprehensive reference lists of prepositions and their use, of verbs with their cases and constructions, of adverbial participles with their shades of meaning and their use. There is also a glossary of grammatical terms and an easy-to-use index.

Acknowledgements

The author wishes to thank Harry Ferrar for his meticulous reading of the manuscript and his many useful suggestions, and the editorial staff of Oxford University Press for their continued support, advice, and encouragement.

Contents

I Verbs

TENSE FORMATION

There are three types of German verb, *weak* (completely regular), *strong* (irregular, though tending to follow certain patterns), and *mixed* (partly strong, partly weak). All German verbs have infinitives ending **-en** (or occasionally just **-n**), so it is not possible to tell from the infinitive of a verb whether it is weak, strong, or mixed.

The tenses of German verbs are either simple, in which case the verb is a single word, or compound, in which case the verb is formed with part of one of the three auxiliary (helping) verbs, **haben**, **sein**, and **werden**, together with the past participle or the infinitive:

> simple tense: **ich sage**, *I say*
> compound tenses: **ich habe gesagt**, *I have said*
> **ich werde sagen**, *I shall say*

Apart from the formation of their past participles, all verbs follow the same pattern in their compound tenses.

Weak verbs

The vast majority of German verbs are weak and follow a single pattern. Their past tense is formed by adding **-te** to their stem (the infinitive minus its **-(e)n** ending), and their past participle is formed **ge . . . t**:

> **sagen**, *to say*
> **ich sage**, *I say*
> **ich sagte**, *I said*
> **ich habe gesagt**, *I have said*

▶ The complete tense formation of a weak (regular) verb is given on pp. 5–7, with the verb endings printed in bold.

▶ Some weak verbs have an infinitive ending **-eln** or **-ern** rather than **-en**. Their endings are dealt with on p. 13.

▶ Some verbs have no **ge-** in their past participle. See p. 14 (Verbs ending **-ieren** and **-eien**) and p. 34 (Inseparable Prefixes).

Strong verbs

Strong verbs change their stem vowels in the past tense and (often) in their past participle, and sometimes in parts of the present as well. They may also change the consonant after that vowel. Their past participles are formed **ge . . . en**.

> **singen**, to sing
> **ich singe**, I sing
> **ich sang**, I sang
> **ich habe gesungen**, I have sung

▶ The endings of strong verbs are regular. The complete tense formation of a strong verb is given on pp. 7–9, with the verb endings printed in bold.

▶ The modal verbs, **lassen**, and **werden** have two past participles used in differing circumstances. See pp. 66–7.

▶ There is a list of all German strong and mixed verbs showing their vowel changes on pp. 73–85.

Mixed verbs

There are only nine mixed verbs: **bringen**, to bring, **denken**, to think, **haben**, to have, **kennen**, to know, **nennen**, to name, **rennen**, to run, **senden**, to send, **wenden**, to turn, and **wissen**, to know. They take weak verb endings, but also change their stem vowel (and sometimes the following consonant) like strong verbs:

> **bringen**, *to bring*
> **ich bringe**, *I bring*
> **ich brachte**, *I brought*
> **ich habe gebracht**, *I have brought*

▶ The complete tense formation of a mixed verb is given on pp. 9–11, with the verb endings printed in bold. Mixed verbs and their vowel changes are included in the list of Irregular Verbs on pp. 73–85.

Simple-tense formation

The simple tenses are the present and past tenses and the present and past subjunctive.

To form each simple tense a fixed set of endings is added to the verb's stem. The stem is its infinitive minus **-en** (or **-n**). The ending of the verb corresponds to the subject of the verb:

> **ich sage**, *I say*
> **er sagt**, *he says*
> **wir sagen**, *we say*

The endings are different for strong verbs on the one hand and for weak and mixed verbs on the other. See conjugation tables, p. 5 onwards.

Compound-tense formation

Compound tenses are formed, as in English, from the past participle or the infinitive of the verb, used with an auxiliary verb. The auxiliary verbs in German are **haben**, *to have*, **sein**, *to be*, and **werden**, *to become*. The compound tenses and their formation are as follows:

perfect tense:
  present of **haben** + PAST PARTICIPLE: **er hat gesagt**,
  he has said

pluperfect tense:
  past of **haben** + PAST PARTICIPLE: **er hatte gesagt**, *he had said*

future tense:
  present of **werden** + INFINITIVE: **er wird sagen**, *he will say*

conditional tense:
  past subjunctive of **werden** + INFINITIVE: **er würde sagen**, *he would say*

future perfect tense:
  future of **haben** + PAST PARTICIPLE: **er wird gesagt haben**, *he will have said*

conditional perfect tense:
  conditional of **haben** + PAST PARTICIPLE: **er würde gesagt haben**, *he would have said*

perfect subjunctive:
  present subjunctive of **haben** + PAST PARTICIPLE: **er habe gesagt**, *he has said/may have said*

pluperfect subjunctive:
  past subjunctive of **haben** + PAST PARTICIPLE: **er hätte gesagt**, *he had said/might have said*

Transitive verbs form their past compound tenses with **haben**. Intransitive verbs of motion and the verbs **sein**, *to be*, **werden**, *to become*, and **bleiben**, *to remain*, use the auxiliary **sein** instead of **haben** in compound tenses:

> **er ist gewesen**, *he has been*
> **er war geworden**, *he had become*
> **er wird geblieben sein**, *he will have remained*

With some verbs that use **sein** the 'motion' idea may not be immediately obvious. There is a list of these verbs on p. 16.

The past subjunctive is often substituted for the conditional, and the pluperfect subjunctive is very frequently substituted for the conditional perfect. See p. 24.

▶ For the position of the past participle in the sentence see pp. 217–18.

CONJUGATION OF WEAK VERBS

This is the regular pattern for the active form of most German verbs. For the forms of the passive see p. 29.

In all tenses **sie** (*she*), **es** (*it*), **man** (*one*), and singular nouns are followed by the **er** form of the verb; plural nouns are followed by the **sie** (*they*) form.

infinitive	sag**en**, *to say*
present participle	sag**end**, *saying*
past participle	**ge**sag**t**, *said*
imperative	sag**(e)**, *say* (**du** *form*)
	sag**en** wir, *let's say*
	sag**t**, *say* (**ihr** *form*)
	sag**en** Sie, *say* (**Sie** *form*)

Simple tenses

present tense,	ich sag**e**		wir sag**en**
I say, I am saying	du sag**st**		ihr sag**t**
		Sie sag**en**[1]	
	er sag**t**		sie sag**en**

past tense,	ich sag**te**		wir sag**ten**
I said, I was saying	du sag**test**		ihr sag**tet**
		Sie sag**ten**[1]	
	er sag**te**		sie sag**ten**

---

[1] The polite form of *you* in both singular and plural is **Sie**. See p. 133.

present subjunctive,	ich sage		wir sagen
I say, I may say	du sag**est**		ihr sag**et**
		Sie sagen[1]	
	er sage		sie sagen

past subjunctive,	ich sag**te**		wir sag**ten**
I said, I might say	du sag**test**		ihr sag**tet**
		Sie sag**ten**[1]	
	er sag**te**		sie sag**ten**

Compound tenses

perfect tense,	ich **habe** gesagt		wir **haben** gesagt
I said, I have said,	du **hast** gesagt		ihr **habt** gesagt
I have been saying		Sie **haben** gesagt[1]	
	er **hat** gesagt		sie **haben** gesagt

pluperfect tense,	ich **hatte** gesagt		wir **hatten** gesagt
I had said, I had been	du **hattest** gesagt		ihr **hattet** gesagt
saying		Sie **hatten** gesagt[1]	
	er **hatte** gesagt		sie **hatten** gesagt

future tense,	ich **werde** sagen		wir **werden** sagen
I shall[2] say, I	du **wirst** sagen		ihr **werdet** sagen
shall[2] be saying		Sie **werden** sagen[1]	
	er **wird** sagen		sie **werden** sagen

conditional tense,	ich **würde** sagen		wir **würden** sagen
I should[3] say, I	du **würdest** sagen		ihr **würdet** sagen
should[3] be saying		Sie **würden** sagen[1]	
	er **würde** sagen		sie **würden** sagen

future perfect tense,	ich **werde** gesagt **haben**		wir **werden** gesagt **haben**
I shall[2] have said,	du **wirst** gesagt **haben**		ihr **werdet** gesagt **haben**
I shall[2] have been		Sie **werden** gesagt **haben**[1]	
saying	er **wird** gesagt **haben**		sie **werden** gesagt **haben**

---

[1] The polite form of *you* in both singular and plural is **Sie**. See p. 133.

[2] In English we often use *will* here.

[3] In English we often use *would* here.

conditional perfect tense, *I should*[1] *have said, I should*[1] *have been saying*	ich **würde** gesagt **haben**	wir **würden** gesagt **haben**
	du **würdest** gesagt **haben**	ihr **würdet** gesagt **haben**
	Sie **würden** gesagt **haben**[2]	
	er **würde** gesagt **haben**	sie **würden** gesagt **haben**
perfect subjunctive, *I have said, I may have said*	ich **habe** gesagt	wir **haben** gesagt
	du **habest** gesagt	ihr **habet** gesagt
	Sie **haben** gesagt[2]	
	er **habe** gesagt	sie **haben** gesagt
pluperfect subjunctive, *I had said, I might have said*	ich **hätte** gesagt	wir **hätten** gesagt
	du **hättest** gesagt	ihr **hättet** gesagt
	Sie **hätten** gesagt[2]	
	er **hätte** gesagt	sie **hätten** gesagt

CONJUGATION OF STRONG VERBS

This is the regular pattern of endings for the active form of German strong verbs. As well as adding these endings, strong verbs also change their vowel (and sometimes the following consonant) in the past participle, throughout the past tense, and (sometimes) in the **du** and **er** forms of the present and the imperative. These changes are listed in the Irregular Verb list on pp. 73–85. For the forms of the passive see p. 29.

In all tenses **sie** (*she*), **es** (*it*), **man** (*one*), and singular nouns are followed by the **er** form of the verb; plural nouns are followed by the **sie** form.

infinitive	**fangen**, *to catch*
present participle	**fangend**, *catching*
past participle	**gefangen**, *caught*
imperative	**fang(e)**, *catch* (**du** form)[3]

---

[1] In English we often use *would* here.

[2] The polite form of *you* in both singular and plural is **Sie**. See page 133.

[3] Verbs like **fangen** that take an umlaut in the **du** and **er** forms of the present tense do not use it in the imperative. See p. 26.

	fangen wir, *let's catch*
	fangt, *catch* (**ihr** form)
	fangen Sie, *catch* (**Sie** form)

Simple tenses

present tense, *I catch, I am catching*	ich fange		wir fang**en**
	du fäng**st**		ihr fangt
		Sie fang**en**[1]	
	er fäng**t**		sie fang**en**

past tense, *I caught, I was* *catching*	ich fing		wir fing**en**
	du fing**st**		ihr fing**t**
		Sie fing**en**[1]	
	er fing		sie fing**en**

present subjunctive, *I catch, I may catch*	ich fang**e**		wir fang**en**
	du fang**est**		ihr fang**et**
		Sie fang**en**[1]	
	er fang**e**		sie fang**en**

past subjunctive, *I caught, I might* *catch*	ich fing**e**		wir fing**en**
	du fing**est**		ihr fing**et**
		Sie fing**en**[1]	
	er fing**e**		sie fing**en**

Compound tenses

perfect tense, *I caught, I have* *caught, I have been* *catching*	ich **habe** gefangen		wir **haben** gefangen
	du **hast** gefangen		ihr **habt** gefangen
		Sie **haben** gefangen[1]	
	er **hat** gefangen		sie **haben** gefangen

pluperfect tense, *I had caught, I had* *been catching*	ich **hatte** gefangen		wir **hatten** gefangen
	du **hattest** gefangen		ihr **hattet** gefangen
		Sie **hatten** gefangen[1]	
	er **hatte** gefangen		sie **hatten** gefangen

---

[1] The polite form of *you* in both singular and plural is **Sie**. See p. 133.

future tense,	ich **werde** fangen	wir **werden** fangen
I shall[1] *catch, I*	du **wirst** fangen	ihr **werdet** fangen
shall[1] *be catching*	Sie **werden** fangen[2]	
	er **wird** fangen	sie **werden** fangen

conditional tense,	ich **würde** fangen	wir **würden** fangen
I should[3] *catch, I*	du **würdest** fangen	ihr **würdet** fangen
should[3] *be catching*	Sie **würden** fangen[2]	
	er **würde** fangen	sie **würden** fangen

future perfect tense,	ich **werde** gefangen **haben**	wir **werden** gefangen **haben**
I shall[1] *have caught,*	du **wirst** gefangen **haben**	ihr **werdet** gefangen **haben**
I shall[1] *have been*	Sie **werden** gefangen **haben**[2]	
catching	er **wird** gefangen **haben**	sie **werden** gefangen **haben**

conditional perfect	ich **würde** gefangen **haben**	wir **würden** gefangen **haben**
tense, *I should*[3] *have*	du **würdest** gefangen **haben**	ihr **würdet** gefangen **haben**
caught, I should[3]	Sie **würden** gefangen **haben**[2]	
have been catching	er **würde** gefangen **haben**	sie **würden** gefangen **haben**

perfect subjunctive,	ich **habe** gefangen	wir **haben** gefangen
I have caught, I may	du **habest** gefangen	ihr **habet** gefangen
have caught	Sie **haben** gefangen[2]	
	er **habe** gefangen	sie **haben** gefangen

pluperfect subjunctive,	ich **hätte** gefangen	wir **hätten** gefangen
I had caught,	du **hättest** gefangen	ihr **hättet** gefangen
I might have	Sie **hätten** gefangen[2]	
caught	er **hätte** gefangen	sie **hätten** gefangen

CONJUGATION OF MIXED VERBS

This is the regular pattern for the active form of mixed verbs.
For the forms of the passive see p. 29.

---

[1] In English we often use *will* here.
[2] The polite form of *you* in both singular and plural is **Sie**. See page 133.
[3] In English we often use *would* here.

In all tenses **sie** (*she*), **es** (*it*), **man** (*one*), and singular nouns are followed by the **er** form of the verb; plural nouns are followed by the **sie** form.

infinitive	**kennen**, *to know*
present participle	**kennend**, *knowing*
past participle	**gekannt**, *known*
imperative	**kenn(e)**, *know* (**du** form)
	kennen wir, *let's know*
	kennt, *know* (**ihr** form)
	kennen Sie, *know* (**Sie** form)

Simple tenses

present tense, *I know*	ich **kenne**		wir **kennen**
	du **kennst**		ihr **kennt**
		Sie **kennen**[1]	
	er **kennt**		sie **kennen**
past tense, *I knew*	ich **kannte**		wir **kannten**
	du **kanntest**		ihr **kanntet**
		Sie **kannten**[1]	
	er **kannte**		sie **kannten**
present subjunctive, *I know, I may know*	ich **kenne**		wir **kennen**
	du **kennest**		ihr **kennet**
		Sie **kennen**[1]	
	er **kenne**		sie **kennen**
past subjunctive, *I knew, I might know*	ich **kennte**		wir **kennten**
	du **kenntest**		ihr **kenntet**
		Sie **kennten**[1]	
	er **kennte**		sie **kennten**

---

[1] The polite form of *you* in both singular and plural is **Sie**. See p. 133.

Compound tenses

perfect tense,	ich **habe** gekannt	wir **haben** gekannt
I knew, I have known	du **hast** gekannt	ihr **habt** gekannt
	Sie **haben** gekannt[1]	
	er **hat** gekannt	sie **haben** gekannt

pluperfect tense,	ich **hatte** gekannt	wir **hatten** gekannt
I had known	du **hattest** gekannt	ihr **hattet** gekannt
	Sie **hatten** gekannt[1]	
	er **hatte** gekannt	sie **hatten** gekannt

future tense,	ich **werde** kennen	wir **werden** kennen
I shall know	du **wirst** kennen	ihr **werdet** kennen
	Sie **werden** kennen[1]	
	er **wird** kennen	sie **werden** kennen

conditional tense,	ich **würde** kennen	wir **würden** kennen
I would know	du **würdest** kennen	ihr **würdet** kennen
	Sie **würden** kennen[1]	
	er **würde** kennen	sie **würden** kennen

future perfect tense,	ich **werde** gekannt **haben**	wir **werden** gekannt **haben**
I shall have known	du **wirst** gekannt **haben**	ihr **werdet** gekannt **haben**
	Sie **werden** gekannt **haben**[1]	
	er **wird** gekannt **haben**	sie **werden** gekannt **haben**

conditional perfect tense,	ich **würde** gekannt **haben**	wir **würden** gekannt **haben**
I would have	du **würdest** gekannt **haben**	ihr **würdet** gekannt **haben**
known	Sie **würden** gekannt **haben**[1]	
	er **würde** gekannt **haben**	sie **würden** gekannt **haben**

perfect subjunctive,	ich **habe** gekannt	wir **haben** gekannt
I have known, I may	du **habest** gekannt	ihr **habet** gekannt
have known	Sie **haben** gekannt[1]	
	er **habe** gekannt	sie **haben** gekannt

pluperfect subjunctive,	ich **hätte** gekannt	wir **hätten** gekannt
I had known,	du **hättest** gekannt	ihr **hättet** gekannt
I might have	Sie **hätten** gekannt[1]	
known	er **hätte** gekannt	sie **hätten** gekannt

---

[1] The polite form of *you* in both singular and plural is **Sie**. See p. 133.

Minor irregularities in verbs

Almost all these changes are made to make the verb easier to pronounce.

■ Verbs ending **-den** or **-ten**

Weak verbs ending **-den** or **-ten** always add an extra **e** before an ending that doesn't already begin with **e**:

> **reden**, *to speak* : **du redest**, *you speak*
>
> **antworten**, *to answer* : **ihr antwortet**, *you answered*
>
> **blenden**, *to dazzle* : **es hat geblendet**, *it has dazzled*

Strong verbs ending **-den** or **-ten** do the same, except in the **du** form of the past tense:

> **finden**, *to find* : **du findest**, *you find*
>
> **bitten**, *to ask* : **ihr batet**, *you asked*

but

> **du fandst**, *you found*
>
> **du batst**, *you asked*

In speech the **e** is often omitted in the **du** form of the present (of both weak and strong verbs):

> **du antwortst nicht!**, *you're not answering*

■ Verbs ending in **-[**CONSONANT**]men** and **-[**CONSONANT**]nen**

Verbs (they are all weak) with a consonant followed by **m** or **n** at the end of their stem add an extra **e** before an ending that doesn't already begin with **e**, but only if this would otherwise be impossible to pronounce:

> **atmen**, *to breathe* : **du atmest**, *you breathe*
>
> **regnen**, *to rain* : **es regnete**, *it was raining*

but

> **lernen**, *to learn* : **du lernst**, *you learn* (an extra **e** is not
> necessary for pronunciation)

■ Weak verbs ending **-eln** and **-ern**

The **n** is removed from the infinitive to form the stem and normal endings are then added to this; however, the **e** of the stem may be omitted with verbs ending **-eln** (usually) and **-ern** (sometimes) in the **ich** form of the present and the **du** form of the imperative:

> **angeln**, *to fish*: **ich ang(e)le gern**, *I like fishing*
> **rudern**, *to row*: **ich rud(e)re lieber**, *I prefer rowing*
> **schmeicheln**, *to flatter*: **schmeich(e)le mir nicht!**, *don't flatter me*

Plural endings of these verbs have no **e**:

> **wir angeln**, *we fish*
> **ihr rudert**, *you row*

■ Verbs whose stem ends in an **s** sound

All verbs whose stems end **-s**, **-ß**, **-z**, or **-x** lose the **s** in the ending of the **du** form of the present:

> **hexen**, *to bewitch*: **du hext**
> **heizen**, *to heat*: **du heizt**
> **schießen**, *to shoot*: **du schießt**

In strong verbs with these stems the ending of the **du** form of the past tense is **-est**:

> **du schossest**, *you shot* (in spoken German **du schoßt** is also found)

Note that none of this applies to the stem-ending **-sch**, which has quite regular verb endings after it:

> **wischen**, *to wipe*: **du wischst**

■ Verbs whose stem ends in a vowel or **h**

With both weak and strong verbs whose stems end in a vowel or **h**, the **e** of an **-en** ending disappears in spoken German (and sometimes in printed German too, especially in poetry):

> **einsehen**, *to understand* : „**Das sehn Sie nicht ein**", *'You don't understand that'*

This also applies to infinitives, and to the **-en** ending of the past participles of strong verbs:

> **„Das wollen Sie nicht einsehn"**, *'You don't want to understand it'*
>
> **„Das haben Sie nicht eingesehn"**, *'You didn't understand it'*

It does not apply to the past of weak verbs, where a **t** comes before the **-en** ending:

> **bauen**, *build*: **wir bauten; sie bauten**

■ Verbs ending **-ieren** and **-eien**

Verbs ending **-ieren** and **-eien** have no **ge-** in their past participle. They are all weak:

> **ich habe ihn schon informiert**, *I've already informed him*
>
> **das hat sie prophezeit**, *she prophesied that*

▶ Inseparable verbs also form past participles without **ge-**. See p. 34.

■ Loss of **-e** endings

☐ In spoken German the **-e** ending of the **ich** form of the present almost always disappears. This is shown by an apostrophe when quoting speech:

> **„Ja, ich geh' schon"**, **sage ich**, *'Yes, all right, I'm going', I say*

☐ In spoken German the **-e** ending of the **du** form of the imperative almost always disappears in both weak and strong verbs. They are written in quoted speech without an apostrophe:

> **„Komm gut nach Hause"**, **sagte sie**, *'Get home safely', she said*

This applies also to strong verbs that simply add an umlaut to their vowel in the **du** form of the present: in the imperative they do not add the umlaut, but they may take an **e**:

> **fahren**, *to go*
> > **du fährst**, *you go*
> > **fahr/fahre schneller!**, *go faster!*

However, strong verbs that actually change their vowel in the **du** form of the present (as opposed to simply adding an umlaut) also change it in the **du** form of the imperative. They can never take an **e**:

> **helfen**, *to help*
> > **du hilfst**, *you help*
> > **hilf mir!**, *help me!*

□ The final **e** of verbs ending in **-eln**, **-ern** is never dropped if they have already dropped the **e** of their stem (see p. 13). Nor is it dropped with verbs ending **-[CONSONANT]men** or **-[CONSONANT]nen**, whose stem is unpronounceable without an ending:

> **atmen**, *to breathe*: **atme!**

□ In spoken German the **-e** of the ending of the **ich** and **er** forms of weak verbs in the past tense often disappears before a vowel. This is written with an apostrophe:

> „**Na also, ich sagt' es schon**", *'There you are, I told you so'*

COMPOUND TENSES

▶ For the formation of the compound tenses see p. 3.

Compound tenses formed with sein

Virtually all transitive verbs and reflexive verbs form their past compound tenses with **haben**. So do most intransitive verbs.

However, three groups of intransitive verbs use **sein**:

- Verbs expressing motion, involving change of place

> **er ist heute gefahren**, *he left today*
> **sie ist in das Zimmer getanzt**, *she danced into the room*

If the verb simply expresses the action, rather than change of place, **haben** is usually used:

> **ich habe heute viel geritten**, *I've ridden a lot today*
> **wir haben gestern abend im „Astoria" getanzt**, *we went dancing at the Astoria last night*

- Verbs expressing change of state

> **sie ist aufgewacht**, *she woke up*
> **Großmutter ist gestorben**, *grandmother has died*
> **du bist aber groß geworden**, *you have got big*

In this group are included verbs meaning *to happen* (**geschehen, passieren, vorkommen, vorgehen**).

Werden, *to become*, also takes **sein** when it is used to form the passive:

> **ich bin gefragt worden**, *I have been asked*

See Passive, p. 29.

- The following verbs, where the idea of 'motion' or of 'change of state' seems doubtful or non-existent

> **begegnen** (+ DAT), *meet* (also **sich begegnen**, *meet one another*)
> **bleiben**, *remain*
> **gelingen**, *succeed* (**es ist mir gelungen**, *I succeeded*); also **mißlingen**, *fail*
> **glücken**, *succeed* (**es ist mir geglückt**, *I succeeded*); also **mißglücken**, *fail*
> **sein**, *be*

'Motion' verbs used transitively

Some verbs of motion that are normally intransitive and take
sein can also be used transitively. They then take **haben**.

> **hat er dein Mofa gefahren?**, *has he ridden your
> moped?*

A very few verbs that take **sein** when used intransitively, or
that are compounded from verbs that take **sein**, continue to
use **sein** when they are used transitively. They are

> **loswerden**, *get rid of*
> **eingehen**, *take on*
> **Gefahr laufen**, *run a risk*
> **eine Strecke gehen**, *go some distance*

> **bist du diese Katze immer noch nicht
> losgeworden?**, *have you still not got rid of that cat?*

USE OF TENSES

The present tense

There is only one form of the present tense in German,
corresponding to both the present simple and the present
continuous in English. So **ich gehe** translates both *I go* and *I
am going*. There is no possible translation of *I am going* using
the present participle in German. If the continuing nature of the
action needs to be stressed, **(gerade) dabeisein** is used:

> **ich bin gerade dabei, die letzten Worte zu
> schreiben**, *I'm just writing the last words*

General uses of the present tense

■ As in English the present is used not just to indicate what is
going on at the moment:

> **ich stricke einen Pulli**, *I'm knitting a pullover*

but also what habitually occurs:

> **zum Frühstück esse ich nur Müsli,** *I eat only muesli at breakfast*

■ It can also be used, again as in English, to indicate a future:

> **ich komme gleich,** *I'm coming (I'll come) right away*

This use is more frequent than in English, partly because German has no equivalent to the English form *I'm going to . . .* It is especially used when an adverb already shows that the event is in the future:

> **kommst du morgen?,** *are you coming tomorrow?*
> (**wirst du morgen kommen?** asks about intention: *are you going to (do you intend to) come tomorrow?*).
> See uses of the future tense, p. 22.

■ German uses the present as a past narrative tense (the 'historic present') at least as frequently as English:

> Acht Gestalten, die Gesichter hinter Tüchern und Wollmützen versteckt, **schlendern** langsam zum Haus Nummer 128. Dann ein Krachen! Die Eingangstür **splittert,** mit einem Brecheisen **knacken** die Vermummten das Schloß. Für die Nachbarn ein klarer Fall: Hier **sind** Einbrecher am Werk. Die Polizei, die Minuten später am Tatort **erscheint, denkt** ähnlich. Großräumig **werden** die umliegenden Straßen **gesichert,** die übrigen Beamten **observieren** das Haus. Nach und nach **marschieren** immer mehr Männer in das leerstehende Haus am Gereonswall, einige **haben** sogar ihren Hund dabei.
>
> *(Express)*
>
> *Eight figures with their faces hidden behind scarves and woolly hats strolled slowly up to number 128. Then came a crash. The entrance door splintered—the disguised figures were breaking the lock with a crowbar. For the neighbours it was perfectly clear—burglars were at work here. The police, who appeared at the scene of the crime moments later, thought the same thing. The*

*surrounding streets were made secure over a wide area,
the remaining officers took up watch on the house.
Gradually more and more men trooped into the empty
house in Gereonswall. Some even had their dogs with
them.*

English would be unlikely to continue with the historic present
for so long, and through so many verbs. It would either use the
past throughout, as above, or if the passage started in the
historic present it would probably change back to the past at
'*For the neighbours it was perfectly clear . . .*'

Special uses of the present tense

■ Present tense with **seit** (*for, since*, preposition) and **seitdem**
(*since then*, adverb)

□ With the prepositions *for* and *since*, when an action or state
which started in the past is still going on in the present, English
uses the perfect continuous ('*I have been doing*'); German—
exactly like French in these circumstances—uses a present tense.

> **sie wäscht seit anderthalb Stunden ab**, *she's been
> washing up for an hour and a half*
> **ich warte seit zwanzig nach eins**, *I've been waiting
> since twenty past one*

However, where a series of actions is referred to (as opposed
to one continuing one), a perfect is used, as in English:

> **seit Anfang Juli hat es jeden Tag geregnet**, *it's
> rained every single day since the beginning of July*

and the perfect is normally always used where the statement is
negative:

> **ich habe sie seit vier Wochen nicht mehr
> gesehen**, *I haven't seen her for four weeks*

□ Exactly the same rules apply to the adverb **seitdem**, *since (then)*:

> **und seitdem warte ich hier**, *and since then I've
> been waiting here*

> **seitdem hat es jeden Tag geregnet**, *it's rained every day since*
>
> **ich habe sie seitdem nicht mehr gesehen**, *I haven't seen her since*

■ Present tense with **seitdem** or **seit** (*since*, conjunction)

After the conjunction **seitdem**, *since*, the present tense in German in the **seitdem** clause *always* corresponds to the past continuous in English:

> **ich habe kein einziges Wort mit ihr gewechselt, seitdem sie hier wohnt**, *I haven't exchanged a single word with her since she's been living here*

Seit is also used as a conjunction, though less commonly than **seitdem**.

▶ See also **seit** + past tense, p. 21.

▶ For a fuller treatment of the conjunctions **seitdem** and **seit** see pp. 199–200.

■ Present tense with **kommen**

With **kommen** + infinitive (= *come in order to do something*), German uses a present where English uses a perfect:

> **ich komme, euch zu warnen**, *I've come to warn you*

The past tense and the perfect tense

The past tense

■ In written narrative, the German past tense corresponds exactly to the English past:

> **Das Transportflugzeug stürzte in der Nacht zum Mittwoch kurz nach dem Start von Ramstein nach Frankfurt über einem Wald ab und explodierte.**
> *(Berliner Zeitung)*
> *Shortly after leaving Ramstein for Frankfurt on Tuesday night the aircraft came down over a wood and exploded.*

■ In spoken narrative, both the past tense and the perfect are used with little or no difference in meaning. See p. 22, The narrative perfect.

■ The past tense is used with **seit** (*since; for*) and **seitdem** (*since*, conjunction; *since then*, adverb):

> **ich wartete seit zwanzig nach eins**, *I'd been waiting since twenty past one*
>
> **seitdem sie hier wohnte, hatte ich kein einziges Wort mit ihr gewechselt**, *I hadn't exchanged a single word with her since she'd been living here*

Where English uses the pluperfect continuous (= *I had been doing*) with these expressions, German uses the past tense.

▶ See also **seit** + present tense, p. 20.

▶ For a fuller treatment of the conjunctions **seitdem** and **seit** see pp. 199–200.

The perfect tense

■ The perfect tense has two main uses in German: as a 'true' perfect and as a past narrative tense.

□ The 'true' perfect (= *I have done*)

As often in English, the true perfect is used to speak of something that happened in the past and has some bearing on what is being talked about in the present:

> **hast du meine Pralinen gegessen?**, *have you eaten my chocolates?*

However, German uses the perfect in this way much more rigorously than English does:

> **Bismarck hat die Grundlagen des heutigen deutschen Staats gelegt**, *Bismarck laid the foundations of the present German state*

Where English uses a perfect continuous, a perfect is used in German:

> **was hast du gemacht?**, *what have you been doing?*
> **ich habe gelesen; ich habe auch ferngesehen,**
> *I've been reading; I've been watching television too*

□ The narrative perfect

In conversation and letter-writing English usually uses the past as the narrative tense: in German the perfect is commoner. It is especially predominant in south Germany (and Austria and Switzerland). However, the past tense is also in quite common use, especially in north Germany, and especially with **haben** and **sein**, the modals, and some of the commoner strong verbs (e.g. **kommen, gehen**). Perfect and past tenses will frequently be found mixed within the same sentence, and in most cases either is entirely acceptable. If in doubt, use the perfect.

> **er kam gestern (ist gestern gekommen) und wollte wissen, was hier zu tun war — ich hab' ihm sofort die Tür gezeigt (zeigte ihm sofort die Tür),** *he came yesterday and wanted to know what was to be done—I showed him the door straight away*

Where English uses the past continuous to describe a state of affairs, German tends to use a past tense rather than a perfect, though here too the perfect is by no means impossible:

> **es regnete, und so hab' ich meinen Schirm mitgenommen,** *it was raining, and so I took my umbrella*

The future tense

The future is used much less frequently than in English and the present is usually substituted for it if an adverb with a future meaning is used:

> **ich seh' dich morgen,** *I'll see you tomorrow*

This also applies if there is an adverb clause with a future meaning:

wenn Sie das zu Ende geschrieben haben, bin ich schon längst weg, *when you've finished writing that I'll be long gone*

■ The future may express firm intention:

ich werd' dich morgen sehen, du kannst dich darauf verlassen, *I will see you tomorrow, you can rely on it*

■ The future (and more frequently the future perfect) may express probability, as they sometimes do in English:

ich bekomme keine Antwort — er wird nicht da sein, *I'm getting no reply, he's probably not in*

sie wird den Bus wieder verpaßt haben, *she'll have missed her bus again*

■ The future (and the present) are used as alternatives to the imperative (see p. 27):

du wirst sofort nach Hause gehen! (du gehst sofort nach Hause!), *go home immediately!*

The conditional and conditional perfect tenses

■ The conditional is normally found in the main clause of an 'if' sentence ('*if he came I would go*'). The same is true of the conditional perfect. Where these tenses appear in sentences without an 'if' clause, an 'if' clause is generally to be understood:

das würde ich nicht machen! [wenn ich du wäre], *I wouldn't do that! (if I were you)*

das würde sie sonst nicht tun [wenn das nicht der Fall wäre], *otherwise she wouldn't do it (if that were not the case)*

There are three basic types of 'if' sentence:

□ 'it may happen'

wenn er anruft, fahre ich heute noch (werde ich heute noch fahren), *if he phones I'll go today*

The **wenn** clause has a present, the main clause has a present or a future.

□ 'it might happen'

> **wenn er anrufen würde, würde ich heute noch fahren,** *if he phoned I'd go today*

Both clauses have a conditional (American usage has '*would phone*' in the 'if' clause, exactly parallel to the German). In formal German the past subjunctive may be used in the 'if' clause and, if the verb is strong, in the main clause also:

> **wenn er anriefe, führe ich heute noch**

The apparently past-tense '*phoned*' in English is actually a remnant of our past subjunctive.

In spoken German **sollen** is often used in the **wenn** clause (**wenn er anrufen sollte**).

▶ For the forms of the past subjunctive see pp. 5–11.

□ 'it might have happened but it didn't'

> **wenn er angerufen hätte, wäre ich heute noch gefahren,** *if he'd phoned* (American: '*would have phoned*'), *I'd have gone today*

Both clauses normally have a pluperfect subjunctive. The conditional perfect is sometimes found in the main clause (**würde . . . gefahren sein**).

▶ For the forms of the pluperfect subjunctive see pp. 5–11.

■ In all three types normal order (rather than inversion) is occasionally found in the main clause:

> **wenn er anrufen würde, ich würde heute noch fahren**

■ In all three types, if the 'if' clause comes first, the word **wenn** may be entirely omitted, the verb placed at the head of its clause, and **so** or **dann** (*then*) inserted at the head of the main clause:

ruft er heute an, (so/dann) werde ich heute fahren
hätte er angerufen, (so/dann) wäre ich heute
noch gefahren

So is more literary than **dann**. Both may be omitted and in modern journalism often are; beware of attempting to read such sentences as questions!

■ **Wer**, *anyone who*, and **wenn nicht**, *unless*

Wer is really the equivalent of '**wenn jemand**' and follows the same rules as **wenn** used in 'if' sentences:

> **wer das gesagt hätte, hätte gelügt,** *anyone who*
> *said that would have been lying* (= **wenn jemand**
> **das gesagt hätte, hätte er gelügt**)

Wenn nicht also follows the same rules as **wenn**. Notice the position of the **nicht**:

> **wenn er nicht Geld genug hat, wird er zu Hause**
> **bleiben,** *unless he has enough money he'll stay at home*

THE IMPERATIVE

The imperative is used to give orders or instructions or to express requests.

Formation of the imperative

The imperative has four forms, which are based on the **du**, **wir**, **ihr**, and **Sie** forms of the present tense of the verb, with the verb first and the subject always following in the case of the **wir** and **Sie** forms. The **du** form of the imperative ends in **-e** rather than **-st**.

> **mache (du)!**, *make!*
> **machen wir!**, *let's make!*
> **macht (ihr)!**, *make!*
> **machen Sie!**, *make!*

The subject is usually dropped with the **du** and **ihr** forms, unless the sense is '*you* do it, not someone else'. The final **-e** of the **du** form is often omitted, especially in speech. An apostrophe is not used in this case. The exclamation mark is much more common with the imperative in German than in English, though not absolutely obligatory.

■ Strong verbs with a complete vowel change (not just an added umlaut) in the **du** and **er** forms of the present also make this change in the **du** form of the imperative. The final **-e** is never used with these verbs:

> **geben: du gibst; gib!**
> **fahren: du fährst; fahr(e)!**

Nehmen and **treten**, which also make consonant changes in the **du** and **er** forms of the present, make the same changes in the imperative: **nimm!; tritt!**

Sehen (imperative normally **sieh!**) has the form **siehe!** when giving a reference:

> **siehe Kapitel 3**, *see chapter 3*

■ **Sein** has irregular imperative forms: **sei (du), seien wir, seid (ihr), seien Sie**. The **du** forms of the (highly uncommon) imperative of **werden** and **wissen** are **werde!** and **wisse!**

■ Third-person commands (*let him/her/it/them . . .*) are expressed by using the present tense of **sollen**, the imperative of **lassen**, or (more literary) the present subjunctive of the verb:

> **er soll sofort kommen! / laß ihn sofort kommen! / komme sofort!**, *he is to come immediately*

▶ For the present subjunctive see pp. 5–11.

Alternatives to the imperative

■ The forms **wollen wir machen**, **wir wollen machen**, and **laß(t) uns machen** are frequent alternatives to **machen wir**.

■ **Wollen Sie bitte . . .** is much used as a polite form of command or request:

> **wollen Sie bitte Platz nehmen!**, *would you sit down please*

■ Official language often uses an infinitive or (in military commands) a past participle for the imperative:

> **nicht hinauslehnen!**, *don't lean out*
> **stillgestanden!**, *attention!*

■ A future tense may also be used as an imperative (see p. 23), as may a present tense with future meaning:

> **du machst es gleich!**, *you'll do it now!*

■ The impersonal passive (see p. 71) may also be used with an imperative sense:

> **hier wird nicht geraucht!**, *no smoking here!*

REFLEXIVE VERBS

Reflexive verbs are verbs whose direct or indirect object is the same as their subject (*he dries himself; she allows herself a chocolate*). In German they consist of a simple verb followed by the reflexive pronoun in the accusative or dative.

■ **The reflexive pronouns**

Apart from **sich**, they are the same as the ordinary accusative and dative object pronouns. Here is the present tense of two reflexive verbs showing all the reflexive pronouns in the accusative and dative:

sich trocknen, *dry oneself*	**sich erlauben**, *allow oneself (something)*
ich trockne **mich**	ich erlaube **mir**
du trocknest **dich**	du erlaubst **dir**
er trocknet **sich**	er erlaubt **sich**
wir trocknen **uns**	wir erlauben **uns**

ihr trocknet **euch**	ihr erlaubt **euch**
Sie trocknen **sich**	Sie erlauben **sich**
sie trocknen **sich**	sie erlauben **sich**

Notice that **sich** does not have a capital letter in the **Sie** (*you*) form.

□ The reflexive pronoun corresponding to **man** is **sich**.

□ Reflexive verbs form their compound past tenses with **haben**.

□ The reflexive pronoun normally stands in the same position as other pronouns, in normal order immediately after the verb. In an infinitive phrase it comes first:

> **Sie werden gebeten, sich sofort in die Halle zu begeben**, *you are asked to make your way into the hall immediately*

■ Reciprocal pronouns (*each other*)

Reflexive pronouns in the plural—**uns, euch, sich**—as well as meaning *(to) ourselves, (to) yourselves, (to) themselves*, can also mean *(to) one another* or *(to) each other*. This includes **sich** when it refers to **man** with a plural meaning (*we, you, people*, etc.):

> **wir sehen uns übermorgen**, *we'll see each other the day after tomorrow*
> **sie begegnen sich jeden Abend**, *they bump into each other every evening*
> **man muß sich lieben**, *we must love one another*

If ambiguity might arise, **selbst** is added where the pronoun is reflexive and **gegenseitig** where it is reciprocal:

> **sie fragten sich selbst, ob . . .** , *they asked themselves whether . . .*
> **sie fragten sich gegenseitig, ob . . .** , *they asked each other whether . . .*

Instead of the reciprocal pronoun **einander** may be used:

wir sehen einander übermorgen, *we'll see each other the day after tomorrow*

It is less common than **sich**, except after a preposition, where it must be used. It is always written as one word with the preposition:

seid nett zueinander!, *be nice to each other*

■ A German reflexive verb may correspond to a English one:

du mußt dich waschen, *you must wash yourself*

but often it does not:

du hast dich verfahren, *you've taken the wrong road*
das bilden Sie sich ein, *you're just imagining that*

■ Reflexive verbs are occasionally used in German where English uses a passive (see p. 32):

das läßt sich machen, *that can be done*
das erklärt sich leicht, *that's easily explained*

■ The dative of the reflexive pronoun is often used with the sense of *for me* (etc.) to show involvement:

das werd' ich mir auch besorgen, *I'll get myself that too*
das mußt du dir ansehen, *you must have a look at that*
das kann ich mir denken, *I can well believe that*

▶ See also Pronouns, pp. 132–3.

THE PASSIVE

The passive forms of the tenses are those where the subject of the verb experiences the action rather than performs it (active: *he helped*; passive: *he was helped*).

Formation of the passive

The passive in English is formed with parts of the verb *to be* plus the past participle; in German it is formed in a similar way using parts of the verb **werden**, *to become*, plus the past participle:

> **es wird preiswert verkauft**, *it is being sold at a bargain price*
>
> **es wurde überall anerkannt**, *it was recognized everywhere*

■ The tenses of the passive are:

present passive	**es wird gemacht**, *it is done*
past passive	**es wurde gemacht**, *it was done*
perfect passive	**es ist gemacht worden**, *it has been done*
pluperfect passive	**es war gemacht worden**, *it had been done*
future passive	**es wird gemacht werden**, *it will be done*
conditional passive	**es würde gemacht werden**, *it would be done*

The past participle form of **werden** used when forming the passive is **worden**, not **geworden**:

> **er ist von seiner Firma belohnt worden**, *he was rewarded by his firm*

■ The following tenses and verb forms are virtually never used in the passive:

future perfect (**es wird gemacht worden sein**, *it will have been done*)

conditional perfect (**es würde gemacht worden sein**, *it would have been done*—the pluperfect subjunctive is used instead of this—see p. 24)

imperative

present participle

■ Where subjunctive forms of the passive are needed, **werden** is put into its equivalent subjunctive tense:

> **es wird gemacht → es werde gemacht** (present subjunctive passive)

■ With a passive verb in English *by* indicates either the 'doer' of the action or the instrument used. In German **von** is used for the person doing the action, **durch** for the instrument used:

er ist von seiner Frau ermordet worden, *he was murdered by his wife*

er ist durch Gift ermordet worden, *he was killed by poison*

but note

sie ist von einem Bus überfahren worden, *she was run over by a bus*

—in this sentence the bus is seen as the 'doer' of the action, not as an instrument.

■ The ordinary past participle of a verb when used as an adjective always has a passive meaning, as in English:

eine längst vergessene Zeit, *a long-forgotten time* (the time has *been* forgotten)

■ In English, the indirect object of an active verb may be made into the subject of the corresponding passive verb:

Adrian gave me the book→ I was given the book by Adrian

This is impossible in German. *I was given the book* can be translated using **man**:

man gab mir das Buch (literally: *someone gave me the book*)

but if the 'doer' is mentioned ('*by Adrian*') the active form has to be used in German:

Adrian gab mir das Buch

In the same way, verbs which take the dative in German cannot be used in the passive. *I was helped by Adrian* must become active:

Adrian hat mir geholfen

There *is* an impersonal passive equivalent:

es wurde mir von Adrian geholfen (literally: *it was helped to me by Adrian*)

—but this is clumsy and little used, and should be avoided.

▶ For the passive infinitive see p. 45.

Alternatives to the passive with werden

The passive, whilst not being largely avoided as it is in French, is used in German less frequently than in English. This is especially true of the future passive.

■ **Man** (*one, people*) is frequently used instead:

> **man hat mich angerufen**, *I was phoned up*

■ Sometimes a reflexive verb is used:

> **es hat sich als falsch erwiesen**, *it has been proved false*
>
> **das erklärt sich dadurch, daß . . .** , *that is explained by the fact that . . .*
>
> **das läßt sich machen**, *that can be done*

■ When the passive conveys a state rather than an action **sein** is used instead of **werden**:

> **sie war gut dafür geeignet**, *she was well suited to it*
>
> **der Brief ist auf englisch geschrieben**, *the letter is written in English* (but: **er wurde letzte Woche von mir geschrieben**, *it was written by me last week*)

COMPOUND VERBS

Compound verbs follow the same pattern of tense-endings as simple verbs. They are formed by adding a prefix to the simple verb. This prefix may be either separable (**auf-, an-, zu-**, etc.), or inseparable (**er-, be-, ver-**, etc.), or sometimes separable, sometimes inseparable according to the meaning of the verb (**um-, unter-, durch-**, etc.).

Separable prefixes

Most prefixes are separable, and most separable prefixes can also be used as parts of speech in their own right, usually prepositions (**aus**steigen), but occasionally adverbs (**davon**laufen), nouns (**teil**nehmen), adjectives (**frei**sprechen), infinitives (**stehen**bleiben). A verb with a separable prefix always has the stress on the prefix.

Position of the prefix

■ A separable prefix is found attached to its verb in the infinitive:

> **ich muß aufstehen**, *I have to get up*
> **dürfen wir weggehen?**, *may we go away?*

If the infinitive is used with **zu**, the **zu** is inserted between prefix and verb:

> **ich versuche aufzustehen**, *I'm trying to get up*

■ The prefix also remains attached in the present participle:

> **die aufgehende Sonne**, *the rising sun*

■ Once the verb is used in any of its tenses, however, the prefix separates from it and moves to the end of the clause:

> **ich stehe früh auf**, *I get up early*
> **ich stand auf**, *I got up*
> **geh sofort weg!**, *go away at once!*

If the verb itself is at the end of the clause (as is the case in subordinate order) the prefix and verb join up again:

> **ich weiß nicht, wann wir heute abfahren**, *I don't know when we're leaving today*

■ In the past participle the **ge-** appears between prefix and verb:

> **der Zug ist schon abgefahren**, *the train has already left*

Inseparable prefixes

The prefixes **be-, emp-, ent-, er-, ge-, miß-, ver-, zer-** are always inseparable. The only difference between verbs with these prefixes and simple verbs is that they have no **ge-** in their past participle:

> **verstehen**, *to understand*: **ich habe verstanden**

Inseparable prefixes do not exist as independent words (unlike most separable prefixes). They never take the stress, which always goes on the verb itself.

Prefixes that may be either separable or inseparable

The prefixes **durch-, hinter-, über-, um-, unter-, voll-, wider-, wieder-** are separable with some verbs, inseparable with others. Whether they are being used separably or inseparably can immediately be distinguished in speech by where the main accent is—on the prefix or on the stem of the verb.

Often the same verb has different meanings according to whether the prefix is separable or inseparable. Quite frequently the separable version of the verb will have a literal meaning, the inseparable version a figurative one:

> **übersetzen** (sep.), *ferry across*
> **übersetzen** (insep.), *translate*

This is not, however, always the case: if in any doubt, check in the dictionary.

Double prefixes

■ A separable prefix followed by an inseparable one separates, but the verb has no **ge-** in its past participle:

> **zubereiten**, *to prepare*
> **er bereitet das Mittagessen zu**, *he's preparing lunch*

er versucht, das Mittagessen zuzubereiten, *he's trying to prepare lunch*

er hat das Mittagessen zubereitet, *he's prepared lunch*

■ With the verb **mißverstehen,** *to misunderstand* (which has a double inseparable prefix), the prefixes do not separate, and there is no **ge-** in the past participle; however, in the infinitive with **zu** the **miß-** behaves like a separable prefix: **mißzuverstehen,** and the stress throughout is on **miß-:**

sie miß versteht mich immer, *she always misunderstands me*

um mich nicht miß zuverstehen . . . , *so as not to misunderstand me . . .*

■ The separable prefixes **hin-** and **her-** in their literal meanings imply respectively motion away from and motion towards the speaker. As well as being added to simple verbs they may also be added to compound verbs, producing a double separable prefix. This behaves like a single separable prefix:

er kommt herauf, *he's coming up*

er ist heraufgekommen, *he came up*

er braucht nicht heraufzukommen, *he doesn't need to come up*

■ The separable prefix **wieder-** is the equivalent of the English prefix *re-*. Attached to a verb with a separable prefix, it stands alone when the prefix is separated from its verb:

wiederherstellen, *to restore*

ich stelle es wieder her, *I'm restoring it*

stell es wieder her!, *restore it*

sobald du es wiederherstellst . . . , *as soon as you restore it*

man hat es wiederhergestellt, *they've restored it*

man versucht es wiederherzustellen, *they're trying to restore it*

Somewhat similarly, compounds of **sein** and **werden** only join up in their infinitive and past participle:

> **er hofft dazusein**, *he hopes to be present*
> **sobald er da ist**, *as soon as he's there*
> **ich muß es loswerden**, *I must get rid of it*
> **wenn du es endlich los wirst . . .** , *if you're finally getting rid of it . . .*

PARTICIPLES

The present participle

Formation of the present participle

The present participle (in English, the *-ing* part of the verb) is formed in German for all verbs by adding **-d** to the infinitive:

> **machen**, *to make* : **machend**, *making*
> **gehen**, *to go* : **gehend**, *going*

Sein, *to be*, and **haben**, *to have*, have no present participles.

Uses of the present participle

The present participle is most commonly found as an adjective in German, standing immediately in front of a noun:

> **das wartende Auto**, *the waiting car*

It can, in this position, form the last element of a phrase that may be considerably longer than would be possible in front of the noun in English:

> **das reglos in der Hüppertstraße vor den großen Toren der Militärkaserne wartende Auto**, *the car, waiting motionless before the great gates of the military barracks in the Hüppertstraße*

In this position it also substitutes for the infinitive:

> **ein bei dieser Dunkelheit kaum zu sehendes Auto**, *a car scarcely to be seen in this darkness*

Note that the present participle has a passive meaning ('a car to *be* seen') in this construction.

■ Many present participles have come to be treated as adjectives and can be used after verbs such as **sein** or **werden** just as adjectives can. They can equally be used as adverbs. They include

> **auffallend**, *striking*
> **aufregend**, *exciting*
> **reizend**, *charming*
> **empörend**, *shocking*

and noun + present participle combinations such as

> **aufsehenerregend**, *sensational*
> **bahnbrechend**, *pioneering*
> **vielversprechend**, *promising*

> **ich finde sie ganz reizend und überraschend schön,**
> *I find her quite charming and astonishingly beautiful*

The past participle

Formation of the past participle

Past participles of weak verbs are formed by adding **ge-** to the beginning and **-t** to the end of the stem of the verb:

> **machen**, *to make*→**gemacht**, *made*
> **wandern**, *to hike*→**gewandert**, *hiked*

There is an extra **-e** in the past-participle ending of verbs whose infinitives end **-ten** and **-den**:

> **antworten**, *to answer*→**geantwortet**, *answered*
> **senden**, *to send*→**gesendet**, *sent*

Past participles of strong verbs are formed by adding **ge-** to the beginning and **-en** to the end of the stem of the verb, often with a vowel change and sometimes with a consonant change as well:

> **braten**, *to roast* → **gebraten**, *roasted*
> **bleiben**, *to stay* → **geblieben**, *stayed*
> **leiden**, *to suffer* → **gelitten**, *suffered*

▶ The modals and **werden** and **lassen** have two past participles. See p. 30 (**werden**) and p. 66 (modals and **lassen**).

▶ Verbs ending **-eien** and **-ieren** and verbs with inseparable prefixes have no **ge-** in the past participle. For further details see pp. 14 and 34.

▶ For all past participles of strong verbs see the Irregular Verb list, pp. 73–85.

Uses of the past participle

■ The past participle is used to form all the past compound tenses. It is always placed at the end of its clause. See pp. 217–18.

■ The past participle is used with **werden** or **sein** to form the passive. See p. 29.

■ The past participle may be used adjectivally; it then agrees with a following noun, takes an adverb qualification, etc., just like any other adjective:

> **ein verlorener Gegenstand**, *a lost object*
> **ich bin völlig erschöpft**, *I'm completely exhausted*

Like the present participle it may be found, with the appropriate adjective ending, standing before its noun at the end of an adjective phrase. This may sometimes be extremely long:

> **ich muß mich für Ihren gestern per Fax in unserem Münchener Büro erhaltenen Brief herzlich bedanken**, *I must thank you cordially for your letter, received yesterday by fax in our Munich office*

This construction is extremely common in books, newspapers, and letters, but almost never found in spoken German.

■ The past participle may be used in an adjective phrase standing separately from its noun. It usually (but not necessarily) stands at the end of the phrase:

> **auf seinen Regenschirm gestützt, trat er ins Restaurant**, *leaning on his umbrella, he came into the restaurant*
>
> **gequält von einer Schar ihrer Enkelkinder, saß die alte Dame ruhig vorm Ofen und strickte**, *tormented by a crowd of her grandchildren the old lady sat by the stove calmly knitting*

■ The past participle is occasionally used as an imperative. See p. 27.

■ After the verb **kommen**, *to come*, German uses the past participle of a motion verb where English uses the present participle:

> **sie kommt gelaufen**, *she comes running*
> **du kamst herbeigeeilt**, *you came hurrying up*

THE SUBJUNCTIVE

The subjunctive expresses doubt, uncertainty, disagreement, and scarcely exists any longer in English (*if I were you; if that be so; would that he were* are some of the few remaining examples of it). In German, though some of its forms are literary or affected, it is still in constant use in both the written and spoken language.

Its main use is in reported matter, in order to disclaim personal responsibility for what is being said, or at least to distance oneself from it. The subjunctive is much used in newspaper reports. It is by no means obligatory when reporting speech, however, and indeed is rarely used when the reporting verb (**er sagt, er meint**, etc.) is in the present and related tenses (see p. 40).

Formation of the subjunctive

The subjunctive has four forms, present, past (sometimes called the imperfect), perfect, and pluperfect. Their grammatical names do NOT indicate their function—the past subjunctive is not a past tense.

▶ For the subjunctive forms of weak verbs see pp. 5–7.

▶ For the subjunctive forms of strong verbs see pp. 7–9.

▶ For the subjunctive forms of mixed verbs see pp. 9–11.

■ The future subjunctive is little used. It is formed with the present subjunctive of **werden** + infinitive:

ich werde gehen	wir werden gehen
du werdest gehen	ihr werdet gehen
er werde gehen	sie werden gehen

■ There is an almost never used future perfect subjunctive, formed with the present subjunctive of **werden** + the perfect infinitive:

ich werde gegangen sein, etc.

■ The present subjunctive of **sein** is irregular:

ich sei	wir seien
du sei(e)st	ihr seiet
er sei	sie seien

The subjunctive in reported speech

The subjunctive is used in indirect speech largely as a distancing device ('this is what she said, it may or may not be true, I'm not responsible for it'). It is what is said, not the 'saying' verb, that goes into the subjunctive.

If the 'saying' verb is in the present, future, or imperative, the verb that follows is not put into the subjunctive. The same applies if the 'saying' verb is in the perfect but refers to something said in the immediate past.

If it is in any past tense the following verb will normally be in the subjunctive. In German (but not in English) the tense of the subjunctive depends on the tense of the *original direct speech*.

Choice of subjunctive tense in reported speech

■ If the original speech was in the present, the present subjunctive is used to report it (or the past subjunctive, see below). This tense sequence is different from English:

> **sie sagte, daß er gehe**, *she said he was going* (her actual words were 'er geht')

■ If the original speech was in a past tense, the perfect subjunctive is used to report it (or the pluperfect subjunctive, see below). This too does not correspond to English tenses:

> **sie sagte, daß er gegangen sei**, *she said he had gone* (her actual words were 'er ist gegangen')

■ If the original speech was in the future or conditional, the conditional is used to report it, unless it is in the **er** form, in which case the future subjunctive may be used:

> **sie sagte, daß du gehen würdest**, *she said you would go* (her actual words were 'du wirst gehen')

but: **sie sagte, daß er gehen werde/würde**, *she said he would go* (her actual words were 'er wird gehen')

■ Many forms of the present and perfect subjunctive are not obviously subjunctive; in such cases the past subjunctive should be used instead of the present subjunctive, and the pluperfect subjunctive instead of the perfect subjunctive:

> **sie sagte, daß ich es hätte**, *she said I had it* (**habe** would not be obviously subjunctive)
>
> **sie sagte, daß ich es gemacht hätte**, *she said I had done it* (**gemacht habe** would not be obviously subjunctive)

This substitution may sometimes be made even when the other tense is clearly subjunctive (especially in the spoken language, and especially by north Germans), and it is almost always made to avoid the **du** and **ihr** forms of the present subjunctive, which are little used in spoken German.

Also avoided are past subjunctives of strong verbs except the most common ones (e.g. **wäre, hätte, würde,** and the modals). Especially shunned are the irregular past subjunctives (see Irregular Verb list, pp. 73–85).

Dropped daß

In all the above examples the **daß** may be dropped, with normal instead of subordinate word order after the 'saying' word:

sie sagte, ich hätte es gemacht

This form without **daß** is actually the more common, except after a negative (**sie sagte nicht, daß . . .**). Newspaper reports will frequently drop the saying verb as well, after an initial indication of who was speaking. Inserts like '*he added*', '*she continued*', '*it went on*' are often necessary in English to show that reported speech continues: in German the subjunctive demonstrates this clearly:

> **Nach Angaben der Meteorologen in Dahlem gingen bei dem Gewitter auch bis zu fünf Zentimeter große Hagelkörner nieder. In Zehlendorf seien** [not **sind**, so this is also part of the report . . .] **23 Liter Niederschlag je Quadratmeter gemessen worden.**
>
> *(Der Tagesspiegel)*

> *According to information received from the Dahlem weather-forecasters, hailstones up to five centimetres in size also fell during this storm. In Zehlendorf precipitation of 23 litres per square metre was measured, it is claimed.*

'Saying' verbs

All verbs introducing reported matter count as 'saying' verbs. The following is a list of such verbs that may not be obviously of this kind at first glance:

ahnen, *suspect*	**erklären,** *explain*
annehmen, *assume*	**erwarten,** *expect*
denken, *think*	**fragen,** *ask*

fühlen, *feel*	**sich einbilden,** *imagine (falsely)*
fürchten, *fear*	**sich vorstellen,** *imagine*
hoffen, *hope*	**träumen,** *dream*
hören, *hear*	**wünschen,** *wish*
meinen, *think*	**zweifeln,** *doubt*
schreiben, *write*	

Other uses of the subjunctive

■ The past subjunctive of **werden** (**würde**) plus the infinitive is used to form the conditional tense; in the case of **sein**, **haben**, the modals, and some of the commoner strong verbs a past subjunctive is often used instead of a conditional:

> **ich würde sein / ich wäre,** *I would be*

■ The past and pluperfect subjunctive are used in 'if' sentences. See Conditional, p. 24.

■ The subjunctive is used in some set third-person commands (**Gott sei Dank!**, *thank God*; **es lebe die Republik!**, *long live the Republic!*). Otherwise third-person commands are expressed by the present of **sollen** or by the imperative of **lassen**:

> **er soll das tun / laß ihn das tun,** *let him do it*

▶ See Imperative, p. 25.

■ The past subjunctive is frequently used in conversation to tone down a suggestion, to make it more polite:

> **ich weiß, wie das zu schaffen wäre,** *I know how that might be managed*
>
> **das wären dreizehn Mark fünfzig,** *that will be DM 13.50*
>
> **wäre Ihnen das recht?,** *would that be all right?*
>
> **wären Sie damit zufrieden?,** *are you happy with that then?*

English has a variety of strategies for this ('*might*', future for present, '*would*', '*then*', etc.).

Note the similar use, when telephoning, of

> **ich hätte gern mit Herrn X gesprochen,** *could I possibly speak to Herr X?*

■ Subjunctive after **als ob / als wenn,** *as if*

The subjunctive is correctly used after **als ob** and **als wenn** (though in casual speech it may not be). There is a difference in meaning according to the tense used:

> **sie sah aus, als ob sie nicht ganz vertrauenswürdig sei,** *she looked as if she wasn't completely reliable (and it turned out she wasn't!)*

> **sie sah aus, als ob sie nicht ganz vertrauenswürdig wäre,** *she looked as if she wasn't completely reliable (but it turned out she was)*

There is a similar difference between perfect and pluperfect subjunctives (both = *had been*).

The **ob** or **wenn** may be dropped, with inverted instead of subordinate word order after **als.** This is more literary:

> **sie sah aus, als sei sie nicht ganz vertrauenswürdig**

■ The subjunctive is also found after **damit** and **(so) daß,** meaning *so that.* This is a very literary use. More usual is the addition of **können:**

> **halt die Leiter, damit er das Bild aufhängen kann (aufhänge),** *hold the ladder, so that he can (may) hang the picture*

Similarly with **damit . . . nicht,** *lest.* Here **können** is not used:

> **halt die Leiter, damit sie nicht fällt (falle),** *hold the ladder, so it doesn't fall*

■ The subjunctive is sometimes used after **nicht daß,** *not that,* **ohne daß,** *without,* **anstatt daß,** *instead of,* and **zu** ADJECTIVE, **als daß,** *too* ADJECTIVE *to.* It gives a less brusque meaning:

nicht, daß Sie zu alt wären . . ., *not that you're too old . . .*
(rather more polite than **nicht, daß Sie zu alt sind . . .**)

The subjunctive tenses found are the past and pluperfect.

THE INFINITIVE

Infinitives of German verbs end in **-en** or occasionally just **-n**, and correspond to the English *to . . .* form of the verb:

> **machen**, *to make*
> **handeln**, *to act*
> **tun**, *to do*

The infinitive is the 'name' of the verb: it is really a sort of noun and can be used as such, then being given a capital letter like all nouns. Infinitives used as nouns are neuter:

> **das Rauchen ist sicher gefährlich**, *smoking (to smoke) is certainly dangerous*

English often uses the *-ing* form of the verb in this case.

■ Infinitives stand at the end of the clause:

> **ich hoffe, morgen in die Stadt zu fahren**, *I hope to go into town tomorrow*

▶ See Word Order, p. 224.

■ When they have a dependent infinitive, the modal verbs (**dürfen, können, mögen, müssen, sollen, wollen**) use their own infinitive instead of their past participle in past compound tenses. The same applies to **lassen, sehen,** and **hören,** and a few other verbs. See pp. 66–7 and 68–9.

■ The infinitive in German has perfect and passive forms:

> **gemacht haben**, *to have made*
> **gemacht werden**, *to be made*
> **gemacht worden sein**, *to have been made*

These forms are used exactly as their English equivalents are:

> **er hofft, bis dann den Versuch gemacht zu
> haben,** *he hopes to have made the attempt by then*

The infinitive with and without zu

Infinitives usually follow ('depend on') another verb, and as in English they are joined to it by **zu**, *to* or by nothing at all:

> **ich versuche zu schwimmen,** *I'm trying to swim*
> **ich muß schwimmen,** *I must swim*

Whether **zu** is used or not depends on the head verb, not on the infinitive, and it doesn't vary—it is always **versuchen** + **zu** + infinitive, **müssen** + infinitive.

■ Most verbs in fact take **zu**. Only the following do not:

□ The modal verbs: **dürfen, können, mögen, müssen, sollen, wollen.** See p. 60 onwards.

□ **sehen,** *to see*
hören, *to hear*
fühlen, *to feel*
spüren, *to feel, to perceive*

> **ich sah ihn kommen,** *I saw him coming*

Again, English uses the *-ing* form of the verb here.

With these verbs a **'wie . . . '** clause is normally substituted if the infinitive would be in any way qualified:

> **ich sah, wie er langsam um die Ecke kam,** *I saw
> him coming slowly round the corner*

□ **finden,** *to find* (only + **stehen** or **liegen,** *to find standing/lying*)

> **ich fand meine Socken auf dem Tisch liegen,**
> *I found my socks lying on the table*

□ **heißen,** *to bid, to tell . . . to* (literary use)

> **er hieß mich gehen,** *he bade me go (he told me to go)*

□ **lassen,** *to let; to make* (see p. 68)

■ **bleiben, gehen, kommen, schicken, haben** are used without **zu** with certain infinitives, as follows.

□ **bleiben** + 'situation' verb:

> **sitzen bleiben,** *to stay seated*
> **stehen bleiben,** *to remain standing*
> etc.

Occasionally the verb joins up with **bleiben** and becomes a separable prefix: **bestehenbleiben,** *to continue*.

□ **gehen, kommen, schicken,** in cases where the interest is entirely focused on the dependent verb:

> **du gehst aber jetzt schlafen!,** *you really are going to bed now!*
> **kommst du heute abend tanzen?,** *are you coming dancing tonight?*
> **sie hat mich einkaufen geschickt,** *she sent me shopping*

Occasionally the verb joins up with **gehen** and becomes a separable prefix: **spazierengehen,** *to go for a walk*.

□ **haben,** meaning *to have something kept or stored somewhere*:

> **ich habe meine Schuhe im Schrank liegen,** *I've got my shoes in the cupboard*

■ Three verbs sometimes take **zu**, sometimes not: **helfen,** *to help*; **lehren,** *to teach*; **lernen,** *to learn*.

With these verbs an unqualified infinitive has no **zu**, a qualified one has **zu**:

> **sie hilft mir abwaschen,** *she's helping me wash up*
> **hilf mir, dieses schmutzige Geschirr abzuwaschen,** *help me wash up these dirty dishes*

With **lehren** and **lernen** a '**wie . . .**' clause is often substituted in the latter case:

> **sie lehrte mich, wie man Geschirr abwäscht,** *she taught me (how) to wash dishes*

■ After **sein**, **zu** + the infinitive has a passive meaning in German:

> **es war niemand zu sehen**, *there was nobody to be seen* (not '*to see*')
>
> **ist Herr Meyer zu sprechen, bitte?**, *can I speak to Herr Meyer please?* (*is Herr M. to be spoken to?*)

■ After parts of speech other than verbs, the infinitive is used with **zu**:

> **das ist schwer zu sagen**, *that's difficult to say*
>
> **ich sehe keine Möglichkeit, das zu tun**, *I can see no possibility of doing that*
>
> **arbeiten ist besser, als im Liegestuhl zu liegen**, *working is better than lying in a deckchair*

In the last case (after **als**) the infinitive is occasionally found without **zu**.

■ Where the sense allows it the infinitive may also be preceded by **um . . . zu**, meaning *in order to*. Notice the word order (**um** always starts the phrase):

> **ich bin hier, um meine Rechte und die meiner Mitbürger zu verlangen**, *I am here in order to demand my rights and those of my fellow citizens*

An adjective with **zu . . .**, *too*, or **. . . genug**, *enough*, is also followed by **um . . . zu** + infinitive, not just **zu**:

> **er ist alt genug (zu jung), um besser zu wissen**, *he's old enough (too young) to know better*

▶ For the use of the infinitive as an imperative see Imperative, p. 27.

▶ For the use of the comma with the infinitive see Punctuation, p. 231.

OBJECT OF THE VERB

Verbs in German may be followed by a direct (accusative) object, an indirect (dative) object, a preposition plus object, or a combination of these.

Verbs with the accusative

Most verbs taking an accusative object ('transitive' verbs) correspond exactly to English verbs and present no problems. But note

■ **sprechen** means *to speak to* and takes an accusative:

> **darf ich ihn sprechen, bitte?**, *may I speak to him please?*

(**Sprechen mit** + dative can also be used in this sense.)

■ **fragen**, **lehren**, **kosten**, and **nennen** (and its more formal equivalent, **heißen**) have two accusative objects:

> **es kostete mich 300 Mark**, *it cost me DM 300*
> **sie lehrte mich Computerwissenschaft**, *she taught me computer science*
> **frag mich das nicht!**, *don't ask me that*
> **er nannte (hieß) mich einen Dummkopf**, *he called me a fool (the second accusative here is technically a complement)*

Verbs with the dative

■ Some verbs that are transitive in English take a dative (indirect) object in German. Such verbs are

auffallen, *to strike*	**gefallen**, *to please*
begegnen, *to meet*	**gehorchen**, *to obey*
danken, *to thank*	**gleichen**, *to equal;*
dienen, *to serve*	*to resemble*
drohen, *to threaten*	**gratulieren**, *to*
folgen, *to follow*	*congratulate*

helfen, to help	**raten**, to advise
imponieren, to impress	**schaden**, to harm
kündigen, to sack	**schmeicheln**, to flatter
leid tun (das tut mir leid), to hurt	**stehen**, to suit
(miß)trauen, to (dis)trust	**trotzen**, to defy
nutzen/nützen, to benefit; to help	**versichern**, to assure (somebody)
passen, to suit; to fit	**weh tun (das tut mir weh)**, to hurt

es hat mir sehr gefallen, it pleased me a lot

sie ist mir begegnet, she met (= ran into) me

Note that **begegnen** and **folgen** are verbs of motion without a direct object and so form their past compound tenses with **sein**.

■ In addition to the above list, most verbs with the following prefixes take the dative: **bei-, ein-, ent-, entgegen-, nach-, vor-, wider-, zu-**:

sie rief mir nach, she called after me
er stand mir bei, he stood by me

But note that **nachahmen** and **nachmachen**, both meaning to imitate, take the accusative.

■ The verbs **erlauben**, to allow, **glauben**, to believe, **verzeihen**, to forgive, **verbieten**, to forbid, and **befehlen**, to order, have an accusative if the object is a thing:

das glaube ich, I believe that
man erlaubt nichts, nothing is allowed

... but a dative if the object is a person:

ich glaube ihr nicht, I don't believe her
man erlaubte ihm, gleich zu fahren, they allowed him to go straight away

With **antworten**, to answer, a personal object is in the dative, but for an impersonal object **auf** + the accusative is used:

> **ich will dir sofort antworten,** *I want to answer you straight away*

> **ich habe auf deinen Brief schon geantwortet,** *I've already answered your letter*

■ A small number of reflexive verbs take a direct object that is not their reflexive pronoun; the reflexive in this case is a dative:

> **das kann ich mir denken,** *I can imagine that*

The dative reflexive differs from the accusative only in the **mir** and **dir** forms (see p. 27).

Most such verbs are reflexive forms of verbs in the list on pp. 49–50. The following verbs, where the reflexive pronoun is dative, are not:

> **sich einbilden,** *to imagine (wrongly)*
> **sich vornehmen,** *to make up one's mind to*
> **sich vorstellen,** *to imagine, to visualize*

> **stell dir das vor!,** *just imagine that!*

▶ Many impersonal verbs also take a dative. See pp. 70–2.

▶ For dative indicating possession see p. 88.

Verbs followed by a preposition

Most prepositions may be used after verbs. Some verbs take more than one preposition, with different meanings.

The preposition that follows a German verb often differs from that used with the equivalent English verb and must be learned with the verb.

Dative or accusative?

For the case used with literal meanings of prepositions that can take either dative or accusative see pp. 159–60. The case with figurative meanings of these prepositions varies according to the preposition used:

■ **an:**   meaning *in respect of, from, by, in connection with*: dative

es fehlt mir am notwendigen Geld, *I lack the necessary money*

ich leide an der Grippe, *I'm suffering from flu*

ich erkannte ihn an seiner Stimme, *I recognized him by his voice*

das hasse ich an deinem Bruder, *that's what I hate about your brother*

meaning *in the (mental) direction of:* accusative

ich erinnere mich an ihn, *I remember him*

denk an mich, *think of me*

glaubst du an Gott?, *do you believe in God?*

■ **auf:** normally accusative, but note **beruhen auf** + DAT, *be based on,* **bestehen auf** + DAT, *insist on*

■ **in:** dative

■ **über:** normally accusative, but note **brüten über** + DAT, *to brood on,* **stehen über** + DAT, *to have mastered (a topic)*

■ **unter:** dative

■ **vor:** dative

▶ The rules above apply equally to prepositions used after adjectives and after nouns.

▶ For the prepositions used with individual verbs see the list on pp. 53–60.

Verb + preposition + -*ing*

English often makes the -*ing* form of the verb into the object of the preposition:

> *I insist on them going with you*
> *I insist on going with you*

In the first type of example above, where *going* has a different subject from *insist,* German uses the preposition compounded with **da-** followed by a clause beginning **daß:**

> **ich bestehe darauf, daß sie mit euch mitfahren**
> (literally: *I insist on it, that . . .*)

In the second type of example above, where both *insist* and *going* have the same subject, an infinitive phrase may be used instead of the **daß** clause:

> **ich bestehe darauf, mit euch mitzufahren**

or:

> **ich bestehe darauf, daß ich mit euch mitfahre**

If the preposition begins with a vowel, as above, **dar-** and not **da-** is added.

Verbs followed by the genitive

A small number of German verbs, mostly reflexive, are followed by the genitive. They are found mainly in literary or legal language. The commonest are

> **anklagen**, *to accuse of*
>
> **berauben**, *to rob of*
>
> **sich entsinnen**, *to recollect*
>
> **sich erbarmen**, *to take pity on*
>
> **sich erfreuen**, *to enjoy* (e.g. health)
>
> **sich erinnern**, *to remember* (more commonly: **an** + ACC)
>
> **sich rühmen**, *to boast*
>
> **sich schämen**, *to be ashamed of* (more commonly: **wegen** + GEN)
>
> **sich vergewissern**, *to make sure of*
>
> **versichern**, *to assure of*
>
> **sich versichern**, *to secure*
>
> **ich kann Sie meiner Hilfe versichern**, *I can assure you of my help*

ALPHABETICAL LIST OF VERB CONSTRUCTIONS

The list includes the commonest verbs taking the dative and the genitive and the commonest verb + preposition constructions (with their case).

abhängen von + DAT	*be dependent on*
achten auf + ACC	*look after*
achtgeben auf + ACC	*pay attention to*
sich amüsieren über + ACC	*laugh at*
angeln nach + DAT	*fish for*
sich ängstigen um + ACC	*be anxious about*
anklagen + GEN	*accuse of*
sich anpassen + DAT	*adapt oneself to*
anspielen auf + ACC	*allude to*
antworten + DAT	*answer (somebody)*
antworten auf + ACC	*answer (something)*
anwenden auf + ACC	*apply to*
sich ärgern über + ACC	*get annoyed with*
auffallen + DAT	*strike (= occur to)*
auffallen an + DAT	*be striking about*
aufhören mit + DAT	*stop (doing)*
aufpassen auf + ACC	*keep an eye on*
ausschauen nach + DAT	*look out for*
ausweichen + DAT	*get out of the way of*
basieren auf + DAT	*be based on*
bauen auf + ACC	*build on*
sich bedanken für + ACC	*thank for*
befehlen + DAT	*order (somebody)*
befördern zu + DAT	*promote (to the post/rank of)*
begegnen + DAT	*meet*
beitragen zu + DAT	*contribute to*
sich beklagen bei + DAT	*complain to*
sich beklagen über + ACC	*complain about*
beneiden um + ACC	*envy (something)*
berauben + GEN	*rob (somebody) of*
beruhen auf + DAT	*be based on*
beruhigen über + ACC	*reassure about*
sich beschäftigen mit + DAT	*occupy oneself with*
sich beschränken auf + ACC	*restrict oneself to*
sich beschweren bei + DAT	*complain to*
sich beschweren über + ACC	*complain about*

bestehen auf + DAT	*insist on*
bestehen aus + DAT	*consist of*
bestehen in + DAT	*consist in*
sich beteiligen an + DAT	*participate in*
beten um + ACC	*pray for*
betteln um + ACC	*beg for*
sich bewerben um + ACC	*apply for*
sich beziehen auf + ACC	*refer to*
bitten um + ACC	*ask for*
danken + DAT	*thank*
denken an + ACC	*think of*
denken über + ACC or	*think of (= have an opinion of)*
von + DAT	
sich (DAT) **denken**	*imagine*
dienen + DAT	*serve*
dienen zu + DAT	*be (used) for*
drohen + DAT	*threaten*
sich drücken vor + DAT	*get out of*
dürsten nach + DAT	*thirst for*
sich (DAT) **einbilden**	*imagine (wrongly)*
eingehen auf + ACC	*agree to*
sich einsetzen für + ACC	*do what one can for*
einverstanden sein mit + DAT	*be in agreement with*
es ekelt (**mich**) **vor** + DAT	*. . . disgusts (me)*
entkommen + DAT	*escape from*
sich entscheiden für + ACC	*decide in favour of*
sich entschließen zu + DAT	*decide on*
sich entschuldigen bei + DAT	*apologize to*
sich entsinnen + GEN	*recollect*
sich erbarmen + GEN	*take pity on*
sich erfreuen + GEN	*enjoy (e.g. health)*
sich erholen von + DAT	*recover from*
erinnern an + ACC	*remind*
sich erinnern an + ACC	*remember*
erkennen an + DAT	*recognize by*
erkranken an + DAT	*become ill with*

sich erkundigen über + ACC or **nach** + DAT	*enquire about*
erlauben + DAT	*allow (somebody)*
ernennen zu + DAT	*appoint (to the post of)*
erröten über + ACC	*blush at*
erschrecken vor + DAT	*be scared by*
erschrecken über + ACC	*be shocked at*
sich erstrecken auf + ACC	*include*
erzählen über + ACC or **von** + DAT	*tell about*
es fehlt an + DAT	*there's a lack of*
fischen nach + DAT	*fish for (e.g. compliments)*
flehen um + ACC	*plead for*
fliehen vor + DAT	*flee from*
folgen + DAT	*follow*
fragen nach + DAT, **um** + ACC, or **über** + ACC	*ask for*
sich freuen auf + ACC	*look forward to*
sich freuen über + ACC	*be pleased at*
sich fürchten vor + DAT	*be afraid of*
gebrauchen zu + DAT	*use for*
gefallen + DAT	*please*
gefallen an + DAT	*be pleasing about*
gehorchen + DAT	*obey*
gehören + DAT	*belong to*
es geht um + ACC	*it's a matter of*
gelingen + DAT	*succeed*
genügen + DAT	*be enough for*
sich gewöhnen an + ACC	*get used to*
glauben + DAT	*believe (somebody)*
glauben an + ACC	*believe in*
gleichen + DAT	*equal*
graben nach + DAT	*dig for*
gratulieren + DAT	*congratulate*
greifen nach + DAT	*reach for*
halten für + ACC	*consider*

halten von + DAT	*think of; hold an opinion of*
handeln von + DAT	*be about*
es handelt sich um + ACC	*it's a question of*
hassen an + DAT	*hate about*
helfen + DAT	*help*
herrschen über + ACC	*rule over*
hinweisen auf + ACC	*refer to*
hoffen auf + ACC	*hope for*
hören über + ACC or **von** + DAT	*hear about*
sich hüten vor + DAT	*be on guard against*
imponieren + DAT	*impress*
sich interessieren für + ACC	*be interested in*
interessiert sein an + DAT	*be interested in*
sich irren in + DAT	*be mistaken about*
kämpfen um + ACC	*fight for*
kennen an + DAT	*know by*
klagen über + ACC	*grumble about*
kommen zu + DAT	*get around to*
konkurrieren um + ACC	*compete for*
sich konzentrieren auf + ACC	*concentrate on*
sich kümmern um + ACC	*care about*
kündigen + DAT	*sack*
lachen über + ACC	*laugh at*
lauern auf + ACC	*lie in wait for*
leben von + DAT	*live on*
leiden an + DAT or **unter** + DAT	*suffer from*
leid tun + DAT (**es tut mir leid**)	*be sorry*
lesen über + ACC or **von** + DAT	*read about*
mißtrauen + DAT	*distrust*
nachdenken über + ACC	*think about*
nachgeben + DAT	*give way to; give more to*
neigen zu + DAT	*be prone to*
nutzen/nützen + DAT	*benefit; help*
passen + DAT	*suit; fit*
raten + DAT	*advise*
reagieren auf + ACC	*react to*

rechnen auf + ACC	count on
rechnen mit + DAT	reckon with
reden von + DAT	talk about
reden über + ACC	say unpleasant things about
reichen + DAT	be enough for
retten vor + DAT	rescue from
riechen nach + DAT	smell of
sich rühmen + GEN	boast
sagen über + ACC or **von** + DAT	say about
sagen zu + DAT	say to
schaden + DAT	harm
schicken nach + DAT	send for
schießen auf + ACC	shoot at
schimpfen über + ACC	grumble at
schimpfen auf + ACC	swear at
schlagen nach + DAT	hit out at
schmecken + DAT	taste good to
schmecken nach + DAT	taste of
schmeicheln + DAT	flatter
schreiben über + ACC or **von** + DAT	write about
schützen vor + DAT	protect from
schwärmen für + ACC or **von** + DAT	be mad/crazy about
sehen nach + DAT	look like
sich sehnen nach + DAT	long for
sorgen für + ACC	look after
sich sorgen um + ACC	worry about
sprechen über + ACC or **von** + DAT	speak about
stehen + DAT	suit
sterben an + DAT	die of (e.g. a disease)
sterben vor + DAT	be dying of (e.g. boredom)
strahlen vor + DAT	beam with
streben nach + DAT	strive for
streiken um + ACC	strike for

sich streiten um + ACC	quarrel over
sich streiten über + ACC	quarrel about
sich stürzen auf + ACC	rush at
suchen nach + DAT	look for
tasten nach + DAT	grope for
sich täuschen über + ACC	be mistaken about
sich täuschen in + DAT	be mistaken in (somebody)
teilnehmen an + DAT	take part in
telefonieren mit + DAT	telephone
telefonieren nach + DAT	telephone for
trauen + DAT	trust
trauern um + ACC	mourn for
träumen von + DAT	dream about
trinken auf + ACC	drink to
trotzen + DAT	defy
überreden zu + DAT	talk into having
sich umsehen nach + DAT	look out for
sich unterhalten über + ACC	talk about
sich verabschieden von + DAT	say goodbye to
verbieten + DAT	forbid (somebody)
verfügen über + ACC	have at one's disposal
sich vergewissern + GEN	make sure of
verlangen nach + DAT	crave for; ask to see
verlängern um + ACC	extend by
sich verlassen auf + ACC	rely on
sich verrechnen um + ACC	make a mistake of
versichern + DAT	assure (somebody)
versichern + GEN	assure . . . of (something)
sich versichern + GEN	make certain of
sich verstecken vor + DAT	hide from
verstehen unter + DAT	understand by
sich verstehen mit + DAT	get on with (somebody)
vertrauen + DAT	trust
verzeihen + DAT	forgive
verzichten auf + ACC	renounce
vorangehen + DAT	go ahead of

vorbeigehen an + DAT	go past
sich vorbereiten auf + ACC	prepare for
sich (DAT) **vornehmen**	make one's mind up
vorstehen + DAT	be in charge of
sich (DAT) **vorstellen**	imagine; visualize
wählen zu + DAT	elect (to the office of)
warnen vor + DAT	warn of
warten auf + ACC	wait for
weh tun + DAT	hurt
sich weiden an + DAT	gloat over
sich wenden an + ACC	turn to
werben um + ACC	court
weitergeben an + ACC	pass on to
widersprechen + DAT	contradict
widerstehen + DAT	resist
wissen über + ACC or **von** + DAT	know about
sich wundern über + ACC	be surprised at
zählen auf + ACC	count on
zählen unter + DAT or **zu** + DAT	number among
sich zanken um + ACC	quarrel over
zielen auf + ACC	aim at
zittern vor + DAT	tremble with
zugrunde gehen an + DAT	be ruined by
zusehen + DAT	watch (somebody)
zustimmen + DAT	agree with

THE MODAL VERBS AND LASSEN

The modal verbs (auxiliary verbs of 'mood' like *can*, *must*, *will* in English) always have a dependent infinitive:

> **darf ich Ihnen helfen?**, *may I help you?*

Even if this infinitive is occasionally not expressed (**darf ich?**, *may I?*), it is virtually always implied. The only exception to this is some uses of **mögen**: see p. 62.

The modal verbs in German are

> **dürfen**, *may* (permission)
> **können**, *can*
> **mögen**, *may* (possibility)
> **müssen**, *must*
> **sollen**, *is to*
> **wollen**, *want*

The meanings given above are in fact not really adequate. These verbs have a number of different meanings and shades of meaning in different uses of their various tenses. These are explained below.

dürfen

■ The basic meaning of **dürfen** is *to be allowed to*; it can also express quite strong possibility. The English equivalent, in both meanings, is often *may* in the present:

> **darf ich Ihnen etwas sagen?**, *may I tell you something?*
> **das darf wohl sein**, *that may well be so*

. . . *could* in the past:

> **ich durfte zum erstenmal reisen**, *I could (= was allowed to) travel for the first time*

. . . and *might* in the past subjunctive:

> **dürfte ich noch ein Stück Torte nehmen?**, *might I possibly take another piece of flan?*
> **das dürfte wahr sein**, *that might well be true*

In the negative, English uses *mustn't = is not allowed to*:

> **das darf ich nicht essen**, *I mustn't (I'm not allowed to) eat that*

■ Note also:

> **was darf es sein?**, *can I help you?; what shall it be? (in shops, bars)*
> **ich darf Ihnen sagen, daß . . .** , *I am able to tell you that . . .*

können

■ Basically **können** corresponds to *can* or *is able to* in the present:

> **kannst du mitfahren?**, *can you come with us?*

. . . and *could* or *was able to* in the past:

> **sie konnte nicht kommen**, *she couldn't come*

■ **Können** also expresses possibility:

> **das kann sein**, *that may be*
> **das kann nicht sein**, *that's not possible*
> **sie kann jeden Moment kommen**, *she may come at any moment*

The past subjunctive expresses remoter possibility:

> **das könnte ich vielleicht tun**, *I might perhaps do that*

■ It is frequently used colloquially for **dürfen**, just as English uses *can* for *may*:

> **kann ich mitkommen?**, *can/may I come with you?*

■ Note also:

> **er kann Italienisch**, *he speaks Italian*
> **dafür kann ich nichts**, *it's not my fault (I can't do anything about it)*

mögen

■ **Mögen** means both *to like*:

> **das mag ich nicht**, *I don't like that*
> **ich mag nicht**, *I don't like to*
> **möchten Sie noch Zucker?**, *would you like some more sugar?*

. . . and *to be likely*, usually expressed by *may* in English:

> **das mag sein**, *that may be*

In the past this becomes, in English, *may (well) have been* or *must have been*:

> **er mochte fünfzig sein**, *he must have been (may well have been) fifty*

■ **Mögen** also means *to want*, with a weaker, more polite sense than **wollen**:

> **ich mochte nicht**, *I didn't want to*

The past subjunctive, **ich möchte**, *I should like*, is much politer than **ich will**, *I want*:

> **ich möchte etwas länger bleiben**, *I should like to stay a little longer*
> **ich möchte Kaffee bitte**, *I should like coffee please*

This is the form of **mögen** in most frequent use.

■ The past subjunctive also expresses polite doubt or disagreement:

> **man möchte vielleicht dagegen einwenden . . .**, *one might just possibly say, on the other hand . . .*

■ The past subjunctive is also used to give polite indirect commands:

> **sagen Sie ihr, Sie möchte hereinkommen**, *tell her to please come in*

müssen

■ The basic meaning of **müssen** is *must* = *to have to*:

> **du mußt alles aufessen**, *you must eat everything up*

In the negative, this becomes *don't have to* in English:

> **du mußt das nicht essen**, *you don't have to eat that*

(*You mustn't eat that!* is correctly **das darfst du nicht essen!** (or **das sollst du nicht essen!**); however, in conversation **du**

mußt das nicht essen is also used in this meaning, with a weaker stress on the **mußt** than in the '*don't have to*' meaning.)

■ **Müssen** is also used to mean *must* or *to have to* expressing inevitability:

> **muß das sein?**, *is that really necessary?*
> **sie muß bald hier sein**, *she's bound to be (she has to be) here soon*

■ **Müssen** in the past subjunctive means *ought to be*, where there is no sense of duty (where there is, **sollte** is used):

> **es müßte gehen**, *it ought to be possible*
> **das Haus müßte irgendwo hier sein**, *the house ought to be somewhere around here*

■ **Haben zu** also exists, meaning *to have to*, where this means *to be in possession of something, to which something must be done*:

> **ich habe ein Auto zu verkaufen**, *I have a car to sell*

but: **ich muß mein Auto verkaufen**, *I have to sell my car*

sollen

■ The basic meaning is *is to* or *is supposed to*, expressing intention:

> **sie soll heute kommen**, *she's to come (supposed to be coming) today*
> **sie sollte gestern kommen**, *she was supposed to be coming yesterday*
> **was soll das heißen?**, *what's that supposed (intended) to mean?*
> **du sollst dein Geld bekommen**, *you're going to get (you're to get) your money*
> **ihr wißt, daß ihr das nicht tun sollt**, *you know you shouldn't (are not supposed to) be doing that*

■ **Sollen** also means *to be supposed to* in the sense of '*people say that*':

er soll reich sein, *he's supposed to be rich*

es soll bis fünf Verletzte gegeben haben, *reports say that up to five people were injured*

■ In the past and pluperfect subjunctive it means *ought to/should* and *ought to have/should have*, expressing moral duty:

das solltest du nicht machen, *you ought not to (shouldn't) do that*

das hätte er nicht tun sollen, *he ought not to (shouldn't) have done that*

■ It is used to express a command or wish, especially in the third person:

er soll ein bißchen warten, *let him wait a bit*

■ It can also be used, like **mögen** (see p. 63), in indirect commands:

sagen Sie ihr, sie soll hereinkommen, *tell her to come in*

wollen

■ The basic meaning of **wollen** is *to want* or *will*:

er will gehen, *he wants to go*

es will nicht funktionieren, *it won't (= refuses to) work*

willst du was?, *do you want something?* (much less polite than **möchtest du etwas?**)

■ **Wollen** also sometimes means *to need*:

das will sehr viel Zeit, *that needs a great deal of time*

■ It frequently means *to be about to*, expressing intention:

das will ich sofort machen, *I'll do that straight away* (stronger than '**das werde ich . . .**')

ich wollte gerade sagen . . ., *I was just going to say . . .*

■ It can form a polite alternative to the imperative:

wollen wir gehen?, *let's go*

wollen Sie bitte Platz nehmen, *would you please take a seat*

■ It can mean *to claim*, or, in the negative, *not to admit*:

er will ein Millionär sein, *he claims to be a millionaire*

kein Mensch will es gemacht haben, *nobody admits they did it*

▶ For **lassen** + an infinitive meaning *to get something done* or *to have something done*, see p. 68.

Formation and use of the modals

▶ The modals are irregular, mixed verbs. For their conjugation see the Irregular Verb list, pp. 73–85.

■ Infinitives dependent on the modals are used without **zu**:

das will ich sofort erklären, *I'll explain that straight away*

■ The modals can also be used without a dependent infinitive:

du mußt nicht, *you don't have to*

das mag ich nicht so sehr, *I'm not too keen on that*

ganz wie du willst, *just as you like*

■ Verbs of motion are very often dropped after the modals, especially in spoken German:

ich will nach Berlin, *I want to go to Berlin*

With **mögen** this can only be done after the past subjunctive, **möchte**.

In the case of separable-prefix verbs, the prefix is not dropped:

ich muß weg (= weggehen), *I must be off*

möchtest du mit? (= mitkommen), *would you like to come with us?*

■ Past participles of the modals

The modal verbs all have two past participles, one formed **ge . . . t**, the other identical with the infinitive. The infinitive form is used where the modal has a dependent infinitive (which is more usually the case):

> **du hast nicht fahren können? — ich habe leider nicht gekonnt**, *you weren't able to go?—I'm sorry, I couldn't*

▶ **Lassen** and, sometimes, **sehen** and **hören** behave similarly. See pp. 68 and 69.

■ Modals in compound tenses in subordinate clauses

When two infinitives come together at the end of a subordinate clause, an auxiliary verb stands before them, not after as you would expect. Where this happens it is usually a modal in a compound tense that is involved:

> **ich weiß, daß du nicht gestern hast fahren können**, *I know you couldn't go yesterday*

Notice that this applies not just with **haben** and **sein** used to form past compound tenses, but also with **werden** in the future and conditional tenses of modals:

> **ich hoffe, daß du nicht wirst spielen müssen**, *I hope you won't have to play*

This whole construction tends to be avoided in conversation (e.g. by using the past tense for the perfect).

■ The modals can be used with a perfect infinitive (past participle plus **haben/sein**), as they can in English. Notice the change in meaning this produces:

> **sie hat es sagen müssen**, *she had to say it*

but: **sie muß es gesagt haben**, *she must have said it*

> **sie haben es machen sollen**, *they were supposed to do it*

but: **sie sollen es gemacht haben**, *they're supposed to have done it*

sie haben es tun können, *they have been able to do it*

but: **sie können es getan haben**, *they may have done it*

■ A modal, as in English, may be followed by a passive infinitive (past participle plus **werden**):

es muß getan werden, *it must be done*

or by another modal:

das mußt du aber machen können, *you really must be able to do that*

Lassen and similar verbs

■ **Lassen** has two principal meanings—*to let*:

er ließ sie entkommen, *he let them escape*

. . . and *to make, to cause to, to have (something done)*:

ich lasse mir die Haare schneiden, *I'm going to have my hair cut*
sie ließ uns holen, *she sent for us (had us fetched)*

■ Like the modal verbs, **lassen** takes a following infinitive without **zu**. Also like the modals, **lassen** has two past participles. They are **gelassen** and **lassen**. The latter is used when **lassen** appears with the infinitive of another verb:

ich habe mir die Haare schneiden lassen, *I've had my hair cut*

■ The reflexive form **sich lassen** means *can be* + past participle. It is followed by an active infinitive in German, with a passive sense:

das läßt sich machen, *that can be done*
es läßt sich nicht leugnen, daß . . . , *it cannot be denied that . . .*

■ The past participles of the compounds **fallenlassen**, *to drop*, and **liegenlassen**, *to leave (lying about)*, are found both with and without **ge-**; the form without **ge-** is the more usual:

wo hast du es denn liegen(ge)lassen?, *where did you leave it then?*

Sehen, hören, heißen, fühlen

■ The rules about infinitives and past participles that apply to **lassen** (infinitives without **zu**; two past-participle forms) also apply to **sehen** and **hören**, where the construction with the infinitive form of the past participle is fairly frequent, especially in written German:

ich habe ihn kommen hören, *I heard him coming*

They also apply to the literary verb **heißen**, *to bid*:

er hieß mich eintreten, *he bade me enter*

■ **Fühlen** takes an infinitive without **zu**; it also has a second past participle in the infinitive form, but this is usually avoided by using **wie**:

ich fühlte mein Herz höher schlagen, *I felt my heart beat faster*
ich habe gefühlt, wie mein Herz höher schlug,
I felt my heart beat faster (**ich habe mein Herz höher schlagen fühlen** is possible but stilted)

▶ For more on these and similar verbs see pp. 46–7.
▶ For **helfen**, **lehren**, and **lernen** with and without **zu**, see p. 47.

IMPERSONAL VERBS

Impersonal verbs are verbs whose subject is, in English, *there* or a non-specific *it*. In German this is **es**:

es ist kein Geld im Safe, *there's no money in the safe*
es regnet, *it's raining*

Impersonal verbs corresponding to English 'it . . . '

With all verbs in this group **es** is seen as a true subject, corresponding to the English *it*. If something other than **es** is put in front of the verb, the **es** is placed after the verb like any normal subject:

> **heute regnet es**, *today it's raining*
> **mich ärgert es, daß . . .** , *it annoys me that . . .*

The **es** also stays in subordinate order:

> **ich weiß nicht, ob es heute regnen wird**, *I don't know if it's going to rain today*

This group includes:

■ Most weather verbs. These have an impersonal *it* (**es**) as subject:

> **es regnet**, *it's raining*
> **es schneit**, *it's snowing*
> **es zieht**, *it's draughty*
> —and very many others

■ Verbs with an impersonal subject and a personal object, either accusative or (more often) dative, sometimes reflexive, for example:

> **es ärgert mich**, *it annoys me*
> **es ist mir recht**, *it's OK by me*
> **es scheint mir**, *it seems to me*
> **es handelt sich um**, *it's a question of*

■ **Es ist** or **es sind** + noun or pronoun. German has a fixed order: normal order with nouns, inversion with pronouns:

> **es ist meine Schwester**, *it's my sister*
> **Sie sind es!**, *it's you!*

Impersonal verbs with a postponed subject (usually corresponding to English 'there . . .')

With these verbs **es** simply functions as a substitute for the real subject, which is being held back until after the verb to give it more importance. This **es** usually corresponds to the English *there*. Very many verbs can be made impersonal in this way:

> **es bleibt jetzt sehr wenig Zeit**, *there's very little time left now*

☐ If the real subject is plural, so is the verb:

> **es stehen viele Autos auf dem Parkplatz**, *there are a lot of cars (standing) in the car park*

☐ If an adverb appears before the verb in this construction, the **es** simply disappears (there is no need for it, as the real subject now takes its normal third place in inverted order):

> **heute stehen viele Autos auf dem Parkplatz**, *there are many cars in the car park today* (compare: **heute regnet es**)

The **es** also disappears in subordinate order, for the same reason:

> **ich weiß schon, daß heute viele Autos auf dem Parkplatz stehen**, *I'm quite aware that there are a lot of cars in the car park today*

▶ For the appropriate translation of *there is* see pp. 72–3.

☐ The real subject may be a clause. Where the real subject is a clause English uses *it* rather than *there* for the 'postponing' subject:

> **es ist wahr, daß er das nie gesagt hat**, *it is true that he never said that* (real subject: *that he never said that*)
>
> **wahr ist, daß er das nie gesagt hat**
>
> **es steht in meiner Zeitung, daß . . .**, *it says in my paper that . . .*
>
> **in meiner Zeitung steht, daß. . .**

☐ With this construction in the passive, no real subject need be expressed at all:

> **es wird hier gebaut / hier wird gebaut**, *there's construction work taking place here*

Impersonal verbs corresponding to an English personal verb

Many German impersonal verbs are the equivalent of ordinary English personal verbs. Among the commonest verbs of this kind are:

>**es fehlt mir an** (+ DAT), *I lack*
>**es geht mir (gut,** etc.**),** *I'm (well, etc.)*
>**es gelingt mir,** *I succeed*
>**es tut mir leid,** *I'm sorry*
>**es freut mich,** *I'm glad*

With verbs in this group the **es** is retained after the verb if anything else is placed first in the sentence:

>**mir geht es gut heute,** *I feel well today*

But note the following exceptions, where the **es** very often disappears, especially in written German:

>**es ist mir (kalt,** etc.**),** *I'm cold, etc.)*
>**es wird mir (kalt,** etc.**),** *I'm getting (cold, etc.)*
>**es ist mir, als ob . . . / es kommt mir vor, als ob . . . ,**
>   *I feel as if . . .*
>**es ist mir schlecht/übel,** *I feel sick*
>**es friert mich,** *I feel cold*
>**es wundert mich, daß . . . ,** *I'm surprised that . . .*
>**mir ist (es) furchtbar warm hier,** *I feel terribly hot here*

In spoken German the **es** is often retained as **'s:**

>**mich friert's,** *I'm cold*

There is, there are

The English expression *there is / there are* corresponds to the German **es ist / es sind,** though German likes to substitute a more precise verb if possible (**es steht, es liegt,** etc.).

However, where existence rather than position is to be expressed, **es gibt** is used instead, meaning *there is, there are*. The **es** is always kept in this construction, the verb is always singular, and it is followed by an accusative:

> **es ist kein einziges Glas im Schrank**, *there isn't a single glass in the cupboard*
>
> **es gibt keine Gläser mehr**, *there aren't any glasses left*

Es ist / es sind loses the **es** in inverted or subordinate order.

ALPHABETICAL LIST OF IRREGULAR VERBS

This list includes all strong and mixed verbs in modern usage.

■ Compound verbs should be looked up under their simple form.

■ Where an irregular present-tense **er** form is given, the same irregularity will occur in the **du** form.

■ Irregular past subjunctives are given in brackets after the past tense.

■ An asterisk before the past participle indicates a verb whose past compound tenses are formed with **sein** when the verb is used intransitively.

▶ For the complete formation of the present and past tenses given here, see pp. 8 and 10.

▶ Past compound tenses and passive tenses are regular (except for the past participle form, given below). For their formation, see pp. 8 and 11 (past compound tenses) and p. 29 (passive tenses).

▶ Future and conditional tenses are regular. For their formation, see pp. 9 and 11.

▶ Present and future subjunctives are regular (except the present subjunctive of **sein**, see p. 40). For their formation see pp. 8 and 10 (present subjunctive) and p. 40 (future subjunctive).

▶ Perfect and pluperfect subjunctives are regular (except for the past participle form, given below). For their formation, see pp. 9 and 121.

▶ Past subjunctives are regular except as shown below, in brackets after the past tense. For their formation see pp. 8 and 10.

infinitive	meaning	present, **er** form, if irregular	past (**er** form; + past subjunctive if irregular)	past participle (* = sein)
backen	bake	backt/bäckt	backte	gebacken
befehlen	command	befiehlt	befahl (beföhle)	befohlen
beginnen	begin		begann	begonnen
beißen	bite		biß	gebissen
bergen	save	birgt	barg	geborgen
bersten	burst	birst	barst	*geborsten
biegen	bend		bog	gebogen
bieten	offer		bot	geboten
binden	tie		band	gebunden
bitten	ask		bat	gebeten
blasen	blow	bläst	blies	geblasen
bleiben	stay		blieb	*geblieben
braten	roast	brät	briet	gebraten
brechen	break	bricht	brach	gebrochen
brennen	burn		brannte (brennte)	gebrannt
bringen	bring		brachte	gebracht
denken	think		dachte	gedacht

infinitive	meaning	present, **er** form, if irregular	past (**er** form; + past subjunctive if irregular)	past participle (*** = sein**)
dreschen	thresh	drischt	drosch	gedroschen
dringen	be urgent		drang	gedrungen
dürfen	be allowed	ich/er darf	durfte	gedurft/dürfen
empfehlen	recommend	empfiehlt	empfahl (empföhle)	empfohlen
erlöschen	die out	erlischt	erlosch	*erloschen
erschrecken	be startled[1]	erschrickt	erschrak	*erschrocken
essen	eat	ißt	aß	gegessen
fahren	travel	fährt	fuhr	*gefahren
fallen	fall	fällt	fiel	*gefallen
fangen	catch	fängt	fing	gefangen
fechten	fence	ficht	focht	gefochten
finden	find		fand	gefunden
flechten	plait	flicht	flocht	geflochten
fliegen	fly		flog	*geflogen
fliehen	flee		floh	*geflohen
fließen	flow		floß	*geflossen
fressen	eat (of animals)	frißt	fraß	gefressen

frieren	freeze		fror	gefroren
gebären	bear (child)	gebärt/gebiert	gebar	geboren
geben	give	gibt	gab	gegeben
gedeihen	prosper		gedieh	*gediehen
gehen	go		ging	*gegangen
gelingen	succeed		gelang	*gelungen
gelten	be valid	gilt	galt (gölte)	gegolten
genesen	recover		genas	*genesen
genießen	enjoy		genoß	genossen
geschehen	happen	geschieht	geschah	*geschehen
gewinnen	win		gewann (gewönne)	gewonnen
gießen	pour		goß	gegossen
gleichen	resemble		glich	geglichen
gleiten	slip		glitt	*geglitten
graben	dig	gräbt	grub	gegraben
greifen	grasp		griff	gegriffen
haben	have	du hast; er hat	hatte	gehabt
halten	hold	hält	hielt	gehalten

---

[1] In the sense of *to startle* **erschrecken** is weak.

infinitive	meaning	present, **er** form, if irregular	past (**er** form; + past subjunctive if irregular)	past participle (* = **sein**)
hauen	*hit*		haute	gehaut/
				gehauen
hängen[1]	*hang*		hing	gehangen
heben	*raise*		hob	gehoben
heißen	*be called*		hieß	geheißen
helfen	*help*	hilft	half (hülfe)	geholfen
kennen	*know*		kannte (kennte)	gekannt
klingen	*sound*		klang	geklungen
kneifen	*pinch*		kniff	gekniffen
kommen	*come*		kam	*gekommen
können	*can*	ich/er kann	konnte	gekonnt/können
kriechen	*crawl*		kroch	*gekrochen
laden	*load*	lädt	lud	geladen
lassen	*let*	läßt	ließ	gelassen/lassen
laufen	*run*	läuft	lief	*gelaufen
leiden	*put up with*		litt	gelitten
leihen	*lend*		lieh	geliehen

lesen	read	liest	las	gelesen
liegen	lie		lag	gelegen
lügen	tell lies		log	gelogen
mahlen	grind		mahlte	gemahlen
meiden	avoid		mied	gemieden
melken[2]	milk	milkt	molk	gemolken
messen	measure	mißt	maß	gemessen
mißlingen	fail		mißlang	*mißlungen
mögen	like	ich/er mag	mochte	gemocht/mögen
müssen	must	ich/er muß	mußte	gemußt/müssen
nehmen	take	nimmt	nahm	genommen
nennen	name		nannte (nennte)	genannt
pfeifen	whistle		pfiff	gepfiffen
preisen	praise		pries	gepriesen
quellen	gush	quillt	quoll	*gequollen
raten	advise	rät	riet	geraten
reiben	rub		rieb	gerieben

[1] Hängen is strong when intransitive, weak when transitive.
[2] Melken is very frequently weak.

infinitive	meaning	present (**er** form), if irregular	past (**er** form; + past subjunctive if irregular)	past participle (* = sein)
reißen	tear		riß	gerissen
reiten	ride		ritt	*geritten
rennen	run		rannte (rennte)	*gerannt
riechen	smell		roch	gerochen
ringen	struggle		rang	gerungen
rinnen	run		rann	*geronnen
rufen	call		rief	gerufen
salzen	salt		salzte	gesalzen
saufen	drink heavily	säuft	soff	gesoffen
saugen[1]	suck		sog	gesogen
schaffen	create[2]		schuf	geschaffen
scheiden	separate		schied	*geschieden
scheinen	seem		schien	geschienen
scheißen	shit		schiß	geschissen
schelten	scold	schilt	schalt (schölte)	gescholten
scheren	trim		schor	geschoren
schieben	push		schob	geschoben

schießen	shoot	schoß	geschossen
schinden	ill-treat	schindete	geschunden
schlafen	sleep	schläft	schlief	geschlafen
schlagen	hit	schlägt	schlug	geschlagen
schleichen	creep		schlich	*geschlichen
schleifen	sharpen		schliff	geschliffen
schleißen[3]	strip		schliß	geschlissen
schließen	shut		schloß	geschlossen
schlingen	loop		schlang	geschlungen
schmeißen	fling		schmiß	geschmissen
schmelzen	melt	schmilzt	schmolz	*geschmolzen
schneiden	cut		schnitt	geschnitten
schreiben	write		schrieb	geschrieben
schreien	shout		schrie	geschrie(e)n
schreiten	step		schritt	*geschritten
schweigen	be silent		schwieg	geschwiegen

---

1 **Saugen** is usually weak.

2 In the sense of *to manage* **schaffen** is weak.

3 **Schleißen** and its compounds are often weak.

infinitive	meaning	present, **er** form, if irregular	past (**er** form; + past subjunctive if irregular)	past participle (* = **sein**)
schwellen	swell[1]	schwillt	schwoll	*geschwollen
schwimmen	swim		schwamm (schwömme)	*geschwommen
schwinden	dwindle		schwand	*geschwunden
schwingen	swing		schwang	*geschwungen
schwören	swear		schwor (schwüre)	geschworen
sehen	see	sieht	sah	gesehen
sein	be	ich bin; du bist; er ist; wir/sie sind; ihr seid	war	*gewesen
senden	send[2]		sandte (sendete)	gesandt
singen	sing		sang	gesungen
sinken	sink		sank	*gesunken
sinnen	think		sann	gesonnen
sitzen	sit		saß	gesessen
sollen	is to	ich/er soll	sollte	gesollt/sollen
spalten	split		spaltete	gespaltet/gespalten

speien	spew forth		spie	gespie(e)n
spinnen	spin		spann (spönne)	gesponnen
sprechen	speak	spricht	sprach	gesprochen
sprießen	sprout		sproß	*gesprossen
springen	jump		sprang	*gesprungen
stechen	stab	sticht	stach	gestochen
stehen	stand		stand (stünde)	gestanden
stehlen	steal	stiehlt	stahl	gestohlen
steigen	climb		stieg	*gestiegen
sterben	die	stirbt	starb (stürbe)	*gestorben
stinken	stink		stank	gestunken
stoßen	push	stößt	stieß	gestoßen
streichen	stroke		strich	gestrichen
streiten	quarrel		stritt	gestritten
tragen	carry	trägt	trug	getragen
treffen	meet	trifft	traf	getroffen

---

[1] In the transitive sense of *to fill (a sail)* **schwellen** is weak.

[2] In the sense of *to broadcast* **senden** is weak.

Infinitive	meaning	present, **er** form, if irregular	past (**er** form; + past subjunctive if irregular)	past participle (* = **sein**)
treiben	drive		trieb	getrieben
treten	step	tritt	trat	*getreten
trinken	drink		trank	getrunken
trügen	deceive		trog	getrogen
tun	do	ich tue; du tust; er/ihr tut; wir/sie tun	tat	getan
verderben	spoil	verdirbt	verdarb (verdürbe)	*verdorben
verdrießen	annoy		verdroß	verdrossen
vergessen	forget	vergißt	vergaß	vergessen
verlieren	lose		verlor	verloren
verlöschen	go out	verlischt	verlosch	*verloschen
wachsen	grow	wächst	wuchs	*gewachsen
waschen	wash	wäscht	wusch	gewaschen
weben[1]	weave		wob	gewoben
weichen	budge		wich	*gewichen
weisen	point		wies	gewiesen

wenden[2]	turn		wandte (wendete)	gewandt
werben	advertise	wirbt	warb (würbe)	geworben
werden	become	du wirst; er wird	wurde	*geworden/worden
werfen	throw	wirft	warf (würfe)	geworfen
wiegen[3]	weigh[3]		wog	gewogen
winden	wind		wand	gewunden
wissen	know	ich/er weiß	wußte	gewußt
wollen	want	ich/er will	wollte	gewollt/wollen
zeihen	indict		zieh	geziehen
ziehen	pull		zog	gezogen
zwingen	force		zwang	gezwungen

[1] Weben is usually weak in modern German.
[2] Wenden may also be weak.
[3] Wiegen is weak when it means *to rock*.

I Articles

Articles are words like *a* and *the*. In German the form of the article changes according to the gender and case of the noun following and according to whether the noun is singular or plural. For noun cases see p. 96.

FORMATION OF ARTICLES

The forms of the definite article (**der**, *the*) and indefinite article (**ein**, *a*) are as follows, shown here with a masculine noun **der Mann**, *man*, a feminine noun **die Frau**, *woman*, a neuter noun **das Buch**, *book*, and a plural noun **die Leute**, *people*:

Definite article: **der**, *the*

	SINGULAR			PLURAL
	masculine	*feminine*	*neuter*	
nominative	der Mann	die Frau	das Buch	die Leute
accusative	den Mann	die Frau	das Buch	die Leute
genitive	des Mannes	der Frau	des Buches	der Leute
dative	dem Mann	der Frau	dem Buch	den Leuten

■ Following the pattern of **der** are: **dieser**, *this/that*; **welcher**, *which*; **jener**, *that*; **jeder**, *every*; **mancher**, *many a*:

dieser, *this, that*

	SINGULAR			PLURAL
	masculine	*feminine*	*neuter*	
nominative	dieser	diese	dieses	diese
accusative	diesen	diese	dieses	diese
genitive	dieses	dieser	dieses	dieser
dative	diesem	dieser	diesem	diesen

▶ **Jener** is uncommon in modern German. For *that* **dieser** or, in speech, an emphasized **der** is used. See Demonstrative Adjectives, p.115.

▶ The definite article often compounds with certain prepositions to form a single word. So **zu + dem = zum**. See p. 161.

▶ For the noun endings in the genitive singular and dative plural, see pp. 97–9.

Indefinite article: **ein**, *a*

	SINGULAR			PLURAL
	masculine	*feminine*	*neuter*	
nominative	ein Mann	eine Frau	ein Buch	keine Leute
accusative	einen Mann	eine Frau	ein Buch	keine Leute
genitive	eines Mannes	einer Frau	eines Buches	keiner Leute
dative	einem Mann	einer Frau	einem Buch	keinen Leuten

■ Following the pattern of **ein** are: **kein**, *no* (used above for the plural forms, since **ein** has no plural) and the possessive adjectives: **mein**, *my*; **dein**, *your*; **sein**, *his/its*; **ihr**, *her/their*; **unser**, *our*; **euer**, *your*; **Ihr**, *your*.

■ **Unser** (sometimes) and **euer** (always) lose the final **e** of their stem when they have an ending: **eure Bücher**.

▶ For **kein** see p. 153.

▶ For the possessives see p. 115.

USING THE ARTICLES

Articles are used in a number of places in German where we would omit them in English.

■ The definite article is used with abstract nouns much more frequently than in English, especially when the noun is generalized:

die Eifersucht ist keine Tugend, *jealousy is no virtue* (jealousy in general)

but: **das klingt wie Eifersucht**, *that sounds like jealousy*
(a bit of jealousy)

Abstract nouns usually lose their definite article after the
prepositions **durch**, *through*, **gegen**, *against*, **ohne**, *without*, and
über, *about*.

■ The definite article, with added emphasis in speech, is used
instead of the demonstrative **jener**, to mean *that*:

ich möchte *den* Kuchen, bitte, *I'd like that cake, please*

■ The definite article is used with a noun in the genitive where
in English no article would be used:

der Klang der Musik, *the sound of music*

Spoken German usually prefers **von** to the genitive; no article is
then necessary:

der Klang von Musik

■ The definite article is often used instead of the possessive
with parts of the body and with clothes:

hebt die Hand!, *put your hand up!*
zieh das Hemd aus, *take your shirt off*

A dative to indicate the person concerned may be added . . .

möchtest du dir die Hände waschen?, *would you
like to wash your hands?*

. . . and must be added when someone other than the subject of
the sentence owns the piece of clothing or the part of the body
referred to:

sie drückte mir die Hand, *she pressed my hand*

□ This construction cannot be used when the part of the body
is the subject:

deine Hand ist sehr klein, *your hand is very small*

□ The alternative construction with the possessive as in
English, though less frequent, is entirely possible:

zieh dein Hemd aus, *take your shirt off*

■ The definite article is used with geographical names in the following instances:

□ Before feminine names of countries:

wir fahren in die Schweiz, *we're travelling to Switzerland*

It is also used with the very few masculine and plural country names. See pp. 93 and 176. The article is dropped in addresses, however: **Schweiz** on the envelope, not **die Schweiz**.

□ Before geographical names with adjectives (English usage varies here):

das neue Deutschland, *the new Germany*
das schöne Italien, *beautiful Italy*

The same applies to proper names:

der doofe Fritz, *daft Fritz*

□ Before names of mountains, lakes, streets:

die Zugspitze; der Comer See, *Lake Como*; **die Bismarckstraße**

■ The definite article is used with months, seasons, parts of the day, meals:

am Vormittag, *in the morning*
der Mai ist gekommen, *May is here*
im Sommer nimmt man das Frühstück draußen,
in summer we eat breakfast outside

■ A definite (not an indefinite) article is used in expressions of price + quantity like *seven marks a kilo*:

sieben Mark das Kilo, *seven marks a kilo*
drei Mark das Stück, *three marks apiece*

Pro, *per*, may also be used in this way. See Prepositions, p. 178.

■ A definite article may be used, familiarly, before proper names:

> **hast du den Günter gesehen?**, *have you seen Günter?*

OMISSION OF THE ARTICLES

■ The article is omitted in many prepositional phrases where we would expect it in English:

> **zu Ende**, *at an end*
> **bei Ausbruch des Krieges**, *at the outbreak of war*
> **nach längerer Zeit**, *after quite a long time*

And note **Anfang**, **Mitte**, and **Ende** with months, where both article and preposition are omitted:

> **sie kommt Anfang September**, *she's coming at the beginning of September*

■ The indefinite article is not used after **sein**, *to be* (or **werden**, *to become*, or **bleiben**, *to remain*) + a profession or nationality:

> **er wird Computerwissenschafler**, *he's going to be a computer scientist*
> **sie ist Amerikanerin**, *she's an American*

It *is* used, though, if there is an adjective in front of the noun:

> **er ist ein bekannter Schriftsteller**, *he's a well-known writer*

■ The indefinite article is not used after **als**, *as (a)*:

> **ich als Engländer weiß, daß . . .** , *I as an Englishman know that . . .*
> **er arbeitet als Maurer**, *he's working as a builder*

I Nouns

All nouns in German are spelled with a capital letter.

GENDER OF NOUNS

English has three genders: masculine, feminine, and neuter (*he, she, it*). German also has three, but whereas in English gender virtually always corresponds logically to the sex of the noun, this is not the case in German. Most nouns denoting male people and animals are in fact masculine in German, most of those denoting females are feminine; but names of inanimate objects may be masculine, feminine, or neuter. Unlike English nouns, German nouns usually make their gender obvious by means of the article and (sometimes) the adjectives in front of them.

The rules for gender in German are far from watertight—there are exceptions to most of them.

Masculine groups

■ Masculine are: names of males; days, months, seasons; points of the compass; makes of car:

> **der Mann**, *man*, **der Montag**, *Monday*, **der Januar**, *January*, **der Sommer**, *summer*, **der Norden**, *north*, **der Opel**

■ Nouns indicating a 'doer', ending **-er**, are masculine:

> **der Gärtner**, *gardener*, **der Sänger**, *singer*

By analogy, so are most 'doing' instruments: **der Computer**, *computer*, **der Wecker**, *alarm*.

■ Nouns ending **-ich**, **-ig**, **-ling** are masculine:

> **der Fittich**, *wing*, **der Honig**, *honey*, **der Lehrling**, *apprentice*

■ Nouns ending **-ismus**, **-ist**, and **-ant** are masculine. These are all of foreign origin:

> **der Kapitalismus**, *capitalism*, **der Bassist**, *bass guitarist*, **der Protestant**, *protestant*

Feminine groups

■ Feminine are: names of females; names of ships, makes of aeroplane; numbers as nouns; German rivers (exceptions: **der Rhein**, **der Main**, **der Neckar**, **der Inn**, **der Lech**). Non-German rivers ending **-a** or **-e** are also feminine; others are masculine:

> **die Frau**, *woman*, **die Scharnhorst**, **die Boeing**, **die Sieben**, *(the) seven*, **die Donau**, *Danube*, **die Wolga**, *Volga*, **die Themse**, *Thames*

■ Feminine forms of traders, workers, and many animals are made by adding **-in**:

> **die Gärtnerin**, *gardener*, **die Sängerin**, *singer*, **die Hündin**, *bitch*

Often an umlaut is added where this is possible (as in **Hund→Hündin** above).

■ Nouns ending **-ei**, **-ie**, **-ion**, **-heit**, **-keit**, **-schaft**, **-tät**, **-ung** are feminine (these are mostly abstract nouns):

> **die Gärtnerei**, *gardening*, **die Chemie**, *chemistry*, **die Nation**, *nation*, **die Klugheit**, *cleverness*, **die Einigkeit**, *unity*, **die Errungenschaft**, *achievement*, **die Rarität**, *rarity*, **die Regierung**, *government*

■ Nouns ending **-a** and most (though beware, not all!) nouns ending **-e** are feminine:

> **die Tuba**, *tuba*, **die Klippe**, *cliff*

Neuter groups

■ Neuter are: names of continents, countries, towns, and the German Länder (common exceptions: **die Bundesrepublik Deutschland**, *the Federal Republic*, **die Vereinigten Staaten** (pl.), *the United States*, **die Schweiz**, *Switzerland*, **die Türkei**, *Turkey*, **die Tschechoslowakei**, *Czechoslovakia*):

> **(das) Europa**, *Europe*, **(das) Deutschland**, *Germany*, **(das) Köln**, *Cologne*, **(das) Bayern**, *Bavaria*

Country names that are not neuter always have the article. *To* is **nach** with neuter countries, **in** with masculines, feminines, and plurals.

■ Neuter are names of metals (exceptions: **die Bronze**, *bronze*, **der Stahl**, *steel*); chemicals; letters of the alphabet; fractions:

> **das Eisen**, *iron*, **das Dioxin**, *dioxin*, **das A**, *A*, **das Drittel**, *third*

■ The names of the young of humans and animals are neuter:

> **das Kind**, *child*, **das Baby**, *baby*, **das Lamm**, *lamb*, **das Kalb**, *calf*, **das Junge** (adjectival noun), *cub*

■ Neuter are nouns ending **-lein** and **-chen**. These indicate diminutives:

> **das Fräulein**, *girl*, **das Mädchen**, *girl*

■ Nouns ending **-tum** and **-um** are neuter (exceptions: **der Reichtum**, *wealth*, **der Irrtum**, *mistake*):

> **das Eigentum**, *property*, **das Zentrum**, *centre*

■ Infinitives (and other parts of speech) used as nouns are neuter:

> **das Lachen**, *laughing*

■ Foreign nouns ending **-ment**, **-fon**, **-ett** are neuter:

> **das Experiment**, *experiment*, **das Mikrofon**, *microphone*, **das Parkett**, *(theatre) stalls*

■ Most (but beware, by no means all!) nouns beginning **Ge-** or ending **-nis** are neuter:

> **das Gebäude**, *building*, **das Geheimnis**, *secret*

Gender of compound nouns

Compound nouns have the same gender as the last element of which they are composed:

> **die Stadt**, *town* → **die Großstadt**, *city*
> **das Haus**, *house* → **das Rathaus**, *town hall*
> **der Baum**, *tree* → **der Apfelbaum**, *apple tree*

■ **Teil**, *part* is masculine, but some of its compounds are masculine, some neuter:

der Vorteil, *advantage*	**das Urteil**, *verdict*
der Nachteil, *disadvantage*	**das Gegenteil**, *opposite*
der Anteil, *share*	**das Abteil**, *compartment*

■ **Meter** and its metric-measurement compounds (**Kilometer, Zentimeter**, etc.) though officially neuter are usually treated as masculine.

Nouns with different genders, depending on meaning

der Band, *volume, book*	**die Band**, *band, group*	**das Band**, *tape, ribbon*
der Bund, *union*		**das Bund**, *bundle*
der Erbe, *heir*		**das Erbe**, *inheritance*
der Gehalt, *capacity*		**das Gehalt**, *salary*
der Golf, *gulf, bay*		**das Golf**, *golf*
der Gummi, *eraser*		**das Gummi**, *rubber*
der Heide, *heathen*	**die Heide**, *heath*	
der Hut, *hat*	**die Hut**, *protection*	
der Junge, *boy*		**das Junge**, *cub*

der Kiefer, *jaw*	**die Kiefer**, *pine*	
der Kunde, *customer*	**die Kunde**, *news*	
der Leiter, *leader, head*	**die Leiter**, *ladder*	
	die Mark, *mark (coin)*	**das Mark**, *marrow*
der Messer, *surveyor*		**das Messer**, *knife*
der Militär, *military man*		**das Militär**, *the military*
der Moment, *moment*		**das Moment**, *factor*
der Otter, *otter*	**die Otter**, *adder*	
der Pack, *package*		**das Pack**, *mob*
der Schild, *shield*		**das Schild**, *sign (board)*
der See, *lake*	**die See**, *sea*	
	die Steuer, *tax*	**das Steuer**, *rudder*
der Stift, *peg, drawing-pin*		**das Stift**, *foundation*
der Tau, *dew*		**das Tau**, *rope*
der Tor, *fool*		**das Tor**, *goal, gate*
der Verdienst, *earnings*		**das Verdienst**, *service*
der Weise, *sage*	**die Weise**, *manner, way*	

Gender traps!

The following nouns have genders that look unlikely:

das Fräulein, *girl*	**das Mitglied**, *member*
die Geisel, *hostage*	**die Person**, *person*
das Genie, *genius*	**die Wache**, *guard, sentry*
das Mädchen, *girl*	**die Waise**, *orphan*

CASE OF NOUNS

Nouns and pronouns are used in four cases in German: the nominative, the accusative, the genitive, and the dative.

■ The nominative is used for the subject of the sentence, and also for the complement of the verbs **sein**, *to be,* **werden,** *to become,* **bleiben,** *to remain,* **heißen,** *to be called,* and a few others.

> **der Hund bellte,** *the dog barked*
> **der Hund ist ein Dackel,** *the dog is a dachshund*

■ The accusative is used for the direct object, and after some prepositions (see p. 160). It is also used for definite adverbial expressions of time (see p. 212):

> **er streichelte den Hund,** *he stroked the dog*
> **er ging rund um den Hund,** *he walked around the dog*
> **sie kommt nächsten Mittwoch,** *she's coming next Wednesday*

■ The genitive is the case which shows possession. It is also used after some prepositions (see p. 160), and for indefinite adverbial expressions of time (see p. 213).

> **der Hund meines Mannes,** *my husband's dog*
> **anstatt des Hundes,** *instead of the dog*
> **eines Tages wird es passieren,** *one day it will happen*

In English a genitive may be placed in front of another noun to show possession:

> *Peter's car; my parents' house*

This is only possible in German with personal names (there is no apostrophe); otherwise the genitive follows the noun:

> **Peters Auto; das Haus meiner Eltern**

■ The dative is the indirect-object case; with some verbs the only object is in the dative (see pp. 49–50). It is also used after many prepositions (see pp. 159 and 160) and with many adjectives (see pp. 110–1):

sie gab dem Hund mein Abendessen, *she gave my supper to the dog*
mit dem Hund, *with the dog*
der Hund ist seinem Frauchen sehr gehorsam, *the dog is very obedient to his mistress*

Case changes in nouns

The case of a noun is indicated largely by the preceding article (see p. 86). Nouns also make the following case changes, however:

■ Almost all masculine nouns which form their plural in **-n** or **-en** also add this ending to all cases of the singular except the nominative:

der Russe, *Russian*

	singular	*plural*
nominative	**der Russe**	**die Russen**
accusative	**den Russen**	**die Russen**
genitive	**des Russen**	**der Russen**
dative	**dem Russen**	**den Russen**

Do not be surprised to hear these nouns used without the **-(e)n** in the singular in conversation.

□ Nouns ending **-or** add **-en** in the plural only. Their genitive singular adds **-s**. The stress moves to the **o** in the plural:

der Professor: genitive singular, **des Professors**
plural, **die Professoren**

□ **Herr** adds **-n** throughout the singular (**Herrn**), **-en** in the plural (**Herren**).

□ Seven masculine nouns ending **-e** add **-ns** instead of **-n** in the genitive singular:

der Name, *name*

	singular	plural
nominative	**der Name**	**die Namen**
accusative	**den Namen**	**die Namen**
genitive	**des Namens**	**der Namen**
dative	**dem Namen**	**den Namen**

The other nouns in this group are: **der Buchstabe**, *letter*, **der Friede**, *peace*, **der Funke**, *spark*, **der Gedanke**, *thought*, **der Glaube**, *belief*, and **der Wille**, *will*. All except **der Buchstabe** may occasionally be found with the **-n** in the nominative too:

> **der Friede** or **der Frieden**, *peace*

One neuter, **das Herz**, *heart*, also behaves in this way; it stays as **das Herz** in the accusative, however.

■ All other masculine nouns and neuter nouns add **-s** or **-es** in the genitive singular. The extra **e** is obligatory with nouns already ending in an 's' sound. It is also frequently found with monosyllables and with nouns with their stress on the last syllable:

> **der Gipfel**, *peak*: genitive singular, **des Gipfels**
>
> **der Schuß**, *shot*: genitive singular, **des Schusses** (for ß to **ss**, see p. 235)
>
> **der Baum**, *tree*: genitive singular, **des Baum(e)s**
>
> **das Geschenk**, *present*: genitive singular, **des Geschenk(e)s**

Neuter nouns ending **-nis** add **-ses** in the genitive:

> **das Gefängnis**, *prison*: genitive singular, **des Gefängnisses**

The genitive sounds rather formal in spoken German. Very frequently **von** + dative is substituted:

> **das Haus meiner Eltern→das Haus von meinen Eltern**, *my parents' house*

■ Personal names, both masculine and feminine, add **-s** in the genitive:

Peters Auto; Lauras Auto; Mutters Auto; Kohls Auto

If the name already ends in an 's' sound (**-s, -ß, -x, -z**) it simply adds an apostrophe for the genitive, or, occasionally in written German, **-ens**:

Hans' Auto or **Hansens Auto**

More frequently **von** is used:

das Auto von Hans

Titles in the genitive, except **Herr**, are not declined:

Kanzler Kohls Außenminister, *Chancellor Kohl's Foreign Minister*

Herrn Schmidts Nase, *Herr Schmidt's nose*

■ Masculine and neuter monosyllables formerly added **-e** to their dative singular. This **e** can still be found in some common expressions: **nach Hause**, *home*; **zu Hause**, *at home*; **auf dem Lande**, *in the country*.

■ All nouns except those with plural **-s** or already ending **-n** add **-n** to their dative plural:

der Mann: nominative plural, **die Männer**
dative plural, **den Männern**

■ Adjectives being used as nouns take a capital letter and the appropriate gender; they still change according to case as if they were adjectives (see Adjectives as nouns, pp. 109–10):

der Reisende, *the (male) traveller*
ein Reisender, *a (male) traveller*

■ A noun in apposition goes into the same case as the noun it stands in apposition to:

er war früher bei Robotron, der größten Firma in dieser Stadt, *he used to be with Robotron, the biggest firm in that town* (**Robotron** is in the dative—after **bei**—so **Firma** is also in the dative)

PLURAL OF NOUNS

There are no watertight rules for the formation of the plural in German. As a very general rule, most masculine nouns have plural ⸚e, most feminines -(e)n, most neuters ⸚er. However, the plural really has to learned with the noun. The following are indications of what a plural is likely to be, rather than rules: there are numerous exceptions.

Plural of masculine nouns

Basically ⸚e.

However, about 50 just add -e and do not modify. Among the commonest that do not modify are:

der Arm, *arm*	**der Punkt**, *point*
der Hund, *dog*	**der Ruf**, *cry*
der Laut, *sound*	**der Schuh**, *shoe*
der Monat, *month*	**der Tag**, *day*
der Ort, *place*	**der Versuch**, *attempt*
der Pfad, *path*	

In addition:

- Nouns ending -el, -en, -er → no ending, some modify
- The following → ⸚er (-er in the case of **Geist**)

der Geist, *spirit*	**der Rand**, *edge*
der Gott, *God*	**der Reichtum**, *wealth* (pl. *riches*)
der Irrtum, *mistake*	**der Strauch**, *shrub*
der Mann, *man*	**der Wald**, *forest*
der Mund, *mouth*	**der Wurm**, *worm*

- Nouns ending -e → -n

Many nouns in this category also add the **-n** in the singular. See pp. 97–8.

Additionally, a group of about 50 masculines not ending **-e** form their plural with **-en**. Many of these do not add the **-en** in the singular (e.g. **der Staat**, *state*, **der See**, *lake*, **der Schmerz**, *pain*, **der Vetter**, *cousin*).

Plural of feminine nouns

Basically -(e)n.

All feminine nouns of more than one syllable form their plural this way, except **die Mutter** (˝), *mother*, **die Tochter** (˝), *daughter*, and nouns ending **-nis**, which double their s and add **e**:

>**die Kenntnis**, *(piece of) knowledge*: plural, **die Kenntnisse**

In addition:

■ About 30 monosyllables form their plural with ˝e. Some of the commoner are

die Frucht, *fruit*	**die Nuß**, *nut*
die Hand, *hand*	**die Stadt**, *town*
die Kuh, *cow*	**die Wand**, *wall*
die Maus, *mouse*	**die Wurst**, *sausage*
die Nacht, *night*	

■ Nouns ending **-in** double their **n** before adding **-en**:

>**die Gärtnerin**, *gardener*: plural, **die Gärtnerinnen**

Modern journalistic usage is to spell this plural with a capital **I** in the middle of the word to produce a unisex version of the otherwise strongly masculine-looking **-er** form:

>**die BürgerInnen**, *male and female citizens*

Plural of neuter nouns

Basically ˝er.

Neuters with plural **-er** always modify if possible. In addition:

■ Neuter nouns ending **-el**, **-en**, **-er** → no change (exception: **das Kloster** (˝), *monastery*)

- Nouns ending **-lein, -chen**→no change

- Nouns ending **-nis**→**-nisse**

     das Ereignis, *event*: plural, **die Ereignisse**

- The following five nouns→**-(e)n**

     das Auge, *eye*, **das Bett**, *bed*, **das Ende**, *end*, **das Hemd**, *shirt*, **das Ohr**, *ear*

These neuters add the **-(e)n** in the plural only.

- About 50 monosyllables→**-e**

Among the commonest are:

das Bein, *leg*	**das Recht**, *right*
das Boot, *boat*	**das Schaf**, *sheep*
das Brot, *loaf*	**das Schiff**, *ship*
das Fest, *festival*	**das Schwein**, *pig*
das Gleis, *rail*	**das Spiel**, *game*
das Haar, *hair*	**das Stück**, *piece*
das Heft, *exercise book*	**das Tier**, *animal*
das Jahr, *year*	**das Tor**, *goal*
das Meer, *sea*	**das Zelt**, *tent*
das Paar, *pair*	**das Ziel**, *aim*
das Pferd, *horse*	

Plural of nouns of foreign origin

Where these have been assimilated into the language over many years they follow the rules and indications above; new and relatively new foreign nouns take **-s**. Some hover, e.g. **der Balkon**, *balcony* (pl.: **-s** or **-e**).

Most foreign nouns ending **-o** take **-s**; those ending **-a** usually change it to **-en** in the plural (**das Drama**, *drama*, **die Dramen**; **die Firma**, *firm*, **die Firmen**—but **das Komma**, *comma*, **die Kommas**).

Plural of compound nouns

Compound nouns have the same plural as the last element of which they are composed.

die Stadt (¨e), *city*, so: **die Hauptstadt** (¨e), *capital*

Compounds of **-mann** form their plural with **-leute**:

der Kaufmann, *merchant*: plural, **die Kaufleute**

Exceptions: **der Schneemann** (¨er), *snowman*, **der Staatsmann** (¨er), *statesman*. And notice **der Ehemann**, *husband*: plural, **die Ehemänner** = *husbands*; plural, **die Eheleute** = *married couples*.

Nouns with different plurals for different meanings

das Band, *bond* (**die Bande**); *tape* (**die Bänder**)

die Bank, *bench* (**die Bänke**); *bank* (**die Banken**)

der Block, *alliance* (**die Blöcke**); *pad of paper, block of flats* (**die Blocks**)

die Mutter, *mother* (**die Mütter**); (tech.) *nut* (**die Muttern**)

der Strauß, *ostrich* (**die Strauße**); *bunch of flowers* (**die Sträuße**)

das Wort, *word* (**die Worte**, *connected words*; **die Wörter**, *unconnected words*)

Nouns with no singular form

The following nouns only occur in the plural:

die Leute, *people*
die Ferien, *holidays*
die Eltern, *parents*
die Großeltern, *grandparents*

Other nouns are substituted for a singular: **die Person**, *person*; **der Ferientag**, *day off*; **der Vater**, *father*, **die Mutter**, *mother*, etc. **Der Elternteil** exists for *parent*, but is literary and clumsy.

Singular for plural

■ The following nouns are singular in German and plural in English:

die Brille, *spectacles*	**das Mittelalter**, *the Middle*
der Dank, *thanks*	*Ages*
das Feuerwerk, *fireworks*	**die Schere**, *scissors*
die Hose, *trousers*	**die Treppe**, *stairs*
der Inhalt, *contents*	**die Umgebung**, *surroundings*
der Lohn, *wages*	**die Zange**, *tongs*

Many of the above have plurals with the sense of 'more than one set of':

zwei Treppen hoch, *up two flights of stairs*

■ The following nouns are singular in English and plural in German:

die Kosten, *cost*	**(die) Weihnachten**, *Christmas*
die Möbel, *furniture*	**(die) Ostern**, *Easter*
die Noten, *(sheet) music*	**(die) Pfingsten**, *Whitsun*
die Zinsen, *interest*	

When the three in the right-hand column are the subject of a sentence, however, they are used with a singular verb:

bald kommt Weihnachten, *Christmas will soon be here*

■ Masculine and neuter nouns used as expressions of quantity do not pluralize:

zwei Glas Wein, *two glasses of wine*

Feminine expressions of quantity do:

zwei Flaschen Wein, *two bottles of wine*

Note that *of* is not translated after expressions of quantity.

| Adjectives

In German, an adjective standing in front of a noun adds endings
to show whether that noun is singular or plural, what its gender is,
and what case it stands in. The endings the adjective adds depend
on what sort of article is standing before it. In general, the more
the article tells you about the noun, the less the adjective does.

Adjectives only add an ending if they stand in front of a
noun—adjectives standing after the verb remain unchanged.
Where two or more adjectives stand in front of a noun they
both take the same ending.

ADJECTIVE ENDINGS

Adjectives after der

The adjective endings following the definite article **der**, *the*, are
as follows:

SINGULAR

	masculine	*feminine*	*neuter*
nom.	der ro**te** Hut, *the red hat*	die ro**te** Lampe, *the red lamp*	das ro**te** Buch, *the red book*
acc.	den ro**ten** Hut	die ro**te** Lampe	das ro**te** Buch
gen.	des ro**ten** Hut(e)s	der ro**ten** Lampe	des ro**ten** Buch(e)s
dat.	dem ro**ten** Hut	der ro**ten** Lampe	dem ro**ten** Buch

PLURAL

nom.	die ro**ten** Autos, *the red cars*
acc.	die ro**ten** Autos
gen.	der ro**ten** Autos
dat.	den ro**ten** Autos

■ Like adjectives after **der** are adjectives after: **welcher**, *which*; **irgendwelcher**, *some . . . or other*; **dieser**, *this/that*; **jener**, *that*; **jeder**, *every*; **mancher**, *many a*.

Adjectives after ein

The adjective endings following the indefinite article **ein**, *a*, are as follows:

SINGULAR

	masculine	*feminine*	*neuter*
nom.	ein rot**er** Hut, *a red hat*	eine rot**e** Lampe, *a red lamp*	ein rot**es** Buch, *a red book*
acc.	einen rot**en** Hut	eine rot**e** Lampe	ein rot**es** Buch
gen.	eines rot**en** Hut(e)s	einer rot**en** Lampe	eines rot**en** Buch(e)s
dat.	einem rot**en** Hut	einer rot**en** Lampe	einem rot**en** Buch

PLURAL

nom.	keine rot**en** Autos, *no red cars*
acc.	keine rot**en** Autos
gen.	keiner rot**en** Autos
dat.	keinen rot**en** Autos

■ Like adjectives after **ein** are adjectives after: **kein**, *no*; **irgendein**, *some . . . or other*; and the possessives **mein**, *my*, **dein**, *your*, **sein**, *his, its*, **ihr**, *her, their*, **unser**, *our*, **euer**, *your*, **Ihr**, *your*. Do not be tempted to add **unser** and **euer** to the 'der' group because they end in **-er**!

■ **Irgendein** has no plural form: **irgendwelche** (see p. 151) is used instead.

Adjectives without an article

Adjectives standing in front of a noun but with no preceding article take the following endings. These give much of the information about gender, case, and number that would otherwise be given by the article:

	SINGULAR		
	masculine	*feminine*	*neuter*
nom.	weiß**er** Wein,	frische Milch,	neu**es** Geld,
	white wine	*fresh milk*	*new money*
acc.	weiß**en** Wein	frische Milch	neu**es** Geld
gen.	weiß**en** Wein(e)s	frisch**er** Milch	neu**en** Geld(e)s
dat.	weiß**em** Wein	frisch**er** Milch	neu**em** Geld

	PLURAL
nom.	junge Leute,
	young people
acc.	junge Leute
gen.	jung**er** Leute
dat.	jung**en** Leuten

■ Notice the **-en** genitive form of masculine and neuter
singular. In fact, the genitive forms are usually avoided if
possible, often by using **von**, *of*.

■ The above endings are used on an adjective that follows an
indeclinable word or phrase like

> **ein bißchen**, *a little*
> **ein paar**, *a few*
> **lauter**, *nothing but*
> **mehr/weniger**, *more/less*
> **-lei** words such as **allerlei**, *all kinds of*, **derlei**, *such
> kinds of*

They are also used after names in the genitive:

> **Mutters neues Kleid**, *mother's new dress*

and after numbers:

> **zwei junge Leute**, *two young people*

Adjectives without endings

■ Adjectives when they do not stand before a noun do not
have endings:

> **die Milch ist frisch**, *the milk is fresh*

■ Adjectives ending in **-a** and those formed from town names by the addition of **-er** have no further endings:

> **eine prima Idee**, *a great idea*
> **ein lila Sofa**, *a purple sofa*
> **die Berliner Luft**, *the Berlin air*

Adjectives after indefinites

Indefinite pronoun + adjective

After **nichts**, *nothing*, **(et)was**, *something*, **allerlei**, *all kinds of*, and other indefinite pronouns an adjective has a capital letter. It takes the ending **-es** in the nominative and accusative and the ending **-em** in the dative (the genitive is rarely found):

> **hier ist etwas Gutes**, *here's something good*
> **hast du nichts Interessanteres?**, *have you nothing more interesting?*
> **mit allerlei Gutem**, *with all kinds of good things*

■ If the adjective is itself an indefinite it takes the ending but no capital:

> **etwas anderes**, *something different*

■ With **alles** the endings differ: nominative and accusative: **alles Neue**, *everything new*; dative: **allem Neuen**.

Indefinite adjective + adjective + noun

This construction is almost always found in the plural. With the indefinite adjectives

bestimmte, *certain*	**mehrere**, *several*
einige, *some*	**verschiedene**, *various*
einzelne, *individual*	**viele**, *many*
folgende, *the following*	**wenige**, *few*
gewisse, *certain*	

—and other less common indefinites—endings on both the

indefinite and the adjective are the same: they are, and behave like, two adjectives, their endings determined by what, if anything, stands in front of them:

> **viele alte Leute,** *many old people*
> **die wenigen jungen Leute,** *the few young people*

However, **alle/sämtliche,** *all*, **beide,** *both*, **solche,** *such*, and **manche,** *many*, are followed by an adjective declined as after the plural **die:**

> **alle guten Leute,** *all good people*

Adjectives losing an e

■ Adjectives ending **-el** (always) and **-en, -er** (sometimes) drop the **e** when they have an ending:

> **übel: eine üble Laune,** *a bad mood*
> **finster: ein finst(e)rer Mensch,** *a sinister person*

The **e** of the comparative **-er** ending is never dropped, however:

> **ein schönerer Tag als gestern,** *a finer day than yesterday*

■ An **e** preceded by **-au** or **-eu** is always dropped if the adjective has an ending:

> **sauer: eine saure Miene,** *a cross look*
> **teuer: ein teures Getränk,** *an expensive drink*

■ The adjective **hoch** loses its **c** when it has an ending:

> **ein hoher Turm,** *a high tower*

ADJECTIVES AS NOUNS

All adjectives can be used as nouns, as can present and past participles. They have a capital letter and the adjective endings they would have if they were followed, according to the sense, by **Mann,** *man,* **Frau,** *woman,* or **Ding,** *thing:*

> **ein Reisender**, *a (male) traveller ('travelling man')*
> **eine Reisende**, *a (female) traveller ('travelling woman')*
> **das Gute und das Böse**, *good and evil ('good thing',
> 'evil thing')*

If they have a qualifying adjective it takes the same ending that
they have:

> **mit diesem müden Reisenden**, *with this tired traveller*

If the adjective has an actual noun that it can refer back to it
does not take a capital:

> **ein kleines Glas und ein großes**, *a small glass and
> a large one*

Der Beamte, *official*, formed from an old past participle,
behaves like an adjective. **Der Junge**, *boy*, originally from the
adjective **jung**, *young*, now behaves like a noun; **das Junge**,
cub, however, still behaves as an adjective.

ADJECTIVES WITH THE DATIVE

Many adjectives can be used with a dative noun or pronoun in
German, almost always corresponding to *to* + noun or pronoun
in English. The dative noun or pronoun usually stands before
the adjective.

The commonest such adjectives are:

ähnlich, *similar*	**gehorsam**, *obedient*
(un)angenehm, *(dis)agreeable*	**(gut, übel) gesinnt**, *(well, badly) disposed*
(un)begreiflich, *(in)comprehensible*	**gleich**, *all the same*
behilflich, *helpful*	**lästig**, *troublesome*
(un)bekannt, *(un)familiar, (un)known*	**leicht**, *easy*
dankbar, *grateful*	**nah(e)**, *near*
egal, *all the same*	**nützlich**, *useful*
ergeben, *devoted*	**peinlich**, *embarrassing*
fremd, *unknown*	**schuldig**, *in debt*

schwer, *difficult*
(un)treu, *(un)faithful*
überlegen, *superior*

unmöglich, *impossible*
unterlegen, *inferior*
unzugänglich, *inaccessible*

> **das ist vielen Leuten unbegreiflich**, *that is incomprehensible to many people*
> **wie kann ich Ihnen behilflich sein?**, *how can I help (be helpful to) you?*

ADJECTIVES WITH THE GENITIVE

In literary German a few adjectives are found with a preceding genitive. **Bewußt**, *aware*, **gewiß**, *certain*, **sicher**, *sure*, **würdig**, *worthy*, are the commonest of these; in everyday German **von** + dative is used instead.

COMPARATIVE AND SUPERLATIVE OF ADJECTIVES

Formation of the comparative and superlative

There are two different ways to form the comparative and superlative of adjectives in English, according to the length of the adjective:

> *long: longer* (comparative), *longest* (superlative)
> *extensive: more extensive* (comparative), *most extensive* (superlative)

German forms the comparative and superlative in one way only, with the two endings **-er** (comparative) and **-(e)st** (superlative). There is no equivalent to the English use of *more*, *most* with longer adjectives.

Normal adjective endings are added to a comparative or superlative adjective standing in front of a noun.

■ Example: **leicht**, *easy*

□ Comparative: **leichter**.

> **es ist leichter, als es war**, *it's easier than it was*
> **das ist eine leichtere Aufgabe**, *that's an easier job*

□ Superlative, before a noun or an understood noun: **leichtest-**.

> **das ist die leichteste Aufgabe**, *that's the easiest job*
> **diese Aufgabe ist die leichteste**, *this job is (the) easiest (job)*

□ Superlative, standing alone: **am leichtesten**

> **das Leben ist in den Ländern des Westens am leichtesten**, *life is easiest in the countries of the West*

In the second type of superlative we are comparing aspects of one thing (here, aspects of life) rather than, as in the first one, several things (several jobs).

The extra **e** in the superlative is used (as above) where the word would be difficult or impossible to pronounce without it.

■ Comparative adjectives whose stem ends **-el**, **-en**, or **-er** usually drop the **e** in their stem when they have a further ending:

> **dunkel**, *dark*: **die dunkleren Abende**, *the darker evenings*

◩ The adjectives listed below modify their vowel in the comparative and superlative, thus:

> **alt**, *old*: comparative: **älter**, superlative: **ältest-**

alt, *old*	**krank**, *sick*
arm, *poor*	**kurz**, *short*
dumm, *stupid*	**lang**, *long*
grob, *coarse*	**scharf**, *sharp*
hart, *hard*	**schwach**, *weak*
jung, *young*	**schwarz**, *black*
kalt, *cold*	**stark**, *strong*
klug, *clever*	**warm**, *warm*

Modification is optional for:

blaß, *pale*	**naß**, *wet*
fromm, *pious*	**rot**, *red*
gesund, *healthy*	**schmal**, *narrow*
glatt, *smooth*	

■ The following adjectives have irregular comparatives and/or superlatives:

	comparative	*superlative*
groß, *big*	größer	größt-
gut, *good*	besser	best-
hoch, *high*	höher	höchst-
nah, *near*	näher	nächst-
viel, *much*	mehr	meist-

Mehr, *more*, and **weniger**, *less*, do not take endings:

> **du hast mehr Geld, er hat weniger Geld**, *you have more money, he has less money*

■ The following adjectives, which are always used in front of a noun and never stand alone, have only comparative and superlative forms. In each case the superlative is formed by addng **-st** to the comparative form:

> **äußer-**, *outer* (**äußerst-**, *outermost*)
> **hinter-**, *back* (**hinterst-**, *hindmost*)
> **inner-**, *inner* (**innerst-**, *innermost*)
> **mittler-**, *middle* (**mittlerst-**, *most central*)
> **nieder-**, *inferior* (**niederst-**, *most inferior*)
> **ober-**, *upper* (**oberst-**, *uppermost*)
> **unter-**, *lower* (**unterst-**, *lowest*)
> **vorder-**, *front* (**vorderst-**, *foremost*)

■ Past participles used as adjectives form their comparative with **mehr** and their superlative with **am meisten** or **meist-**:

> **dies ist das am meisten gekaufte Waschpulver /
> das meistgekaufte Waschpulver**, *this is the most (frequently) purchased washing powder*

Using the comparative and superlative

■ After a comparison *than* is **als**; after expressions of equality (and after negated expressions of equality) *as* is **wie**:

> **er ist älter als ich**, *he's older than I am*
>
> **er ist (nicht) so alt wie sie**, *he's (not) as old as she is*

In conversation **wie** ('**älter wie ich**') is very often also heard in the first type of sentence above.

Than ever after a comparative is **denn je**:

> **es ist teurer denn je**, *it's dearer than ever*

■ *More and more* is **immer** + comparative:

> **die Fragen werden immer schwieriger . . .** , *the questions get more and more difficult . . .*
>
> **. . . und immer länger,** . . . *and longer and longer*

■ *The more . . . the more* is **je . . . desto**:

> **je länger ich warte, desto kälter werd' ich**, *the longer I wait the colder I get*

The word order of the main clause is always **desto** + comparative, followed by inverted order. **Um so** may be used instead of **desto**.

■ With quite a number of common adjectives a comparative can be used to mean '*fairly . . .*':

> **eine längere Zeit**, *a fairly long time*
>
> **eine jüngere Dame**, *a relatively young lady*

■ In English, *most* can mean simply '*extremely*', in which case it corresponds to the superlative adverbs **höchst** (not used with monosyllables) or **äußerst**:

> **das ist äußerst nett von Ihnen**, *that's most kind of you*
>
> **es war höchst unangenehm**, *it was most unpleasant*

DEMONSTRATIVE ADJECTIVES

Demonstrative adjectives (*this, that* in English) stand in exactly the same relationship to nouns as definite and indefinite articles do. They are in fact sometimes known as demonstrative articles.

The demonstrative adjectives in German are **dieser**, *this, that,* and **jener**, *that.* They both decline like **der** (see pp. 86–7).

■ **Jener** is uncommon in modern German. **Dieser** is used for both *this* and *that.* Where a differentiation has to be made an emphasized **der** is used for *that* in speech:

> **darf ich *den* Kuchen haben, bitte?,** *may I have that cake please?*

■ **Da** (or **dort**) may be added after the noun, in which case the **der** and the **da** have equal stress:

> **ja, den Kuchen da (dort),** *yes, that cake*

▶ **Dieser**, **jener**, and **der** can also be used as pronouns (= *this one, that one*). See Demonstrative Pronouns, pp. 137–8.

POSSESSIVE ADJECTIVES

The possessive adjectives are

> **mein**, *mine*
>
> **dein**, *your*
>
> **sein**, *his; its*
>
> **ihr**, *her*
>
> **unser**, *our*
>
> **euer**, *your*
>
> **Ihr**, *your* (polite form)
>
> **ihr**, *your*
>
> **das ist mein Freund,** *that is my friend*

They all decline like **ein** (see p. 87); their endings are determined by the gender and case of the noun that follows them.

■ When **unser** and **euer** have an ending the e of the stem is frequently dropped. This is especially the case with **euer**:

> **das ist eure Mutter?**, *that's your mother?*

In the forms **unseren** and **unserem**, **eueren** and **euerem** the second e is often dropped instead, especially in spoken German:

> **wir kamen mit unserm Vater**, *we came with our father*

■ **Euer** with a capital is used for *Your* in titles:

> **Eure Majestät**, *Your Majesty*
> **Eure Eminenz**, *Your Eminence*

■ The genitive forms of the possessive pronoun (singular: **dessen**, **deren**, **dessen**; plural: **deren**) are used instead of the possessive adjective where it is necessary to avoid ambiguity:

> **sie fuhr mit Ilse und ihrem Freund**, *she was travelling with her friend, and with Ilse*
> **sie fuhr mit Ilse und deren Freund**, *she was travelling with Ilse and her (Ilse's) friend* (**deren** is feminine, to agree with **Ilse**)

▶ *My, your, his, her, our, their* are possessive adjectives and stand in front of a noun. *Mine, yours, his, hers, ours, theirs* are possessive pronouns and stand alone. Don't confuse them! For the possessive pronouns in German see pp. 135–7.

THE INTERROGATIVE ADJECTIVE

The interrogative adjective is **welcher**, *which*:

> **welche Jacke ist deine?**, *which jacket is yours?*
> **welchen Jungen meinst du?**, *which boy do you mean?*

Welcher declines like **der**. See p. 86.

■ As well as beginning a direct question, **welcher** + noun can introduce an indirect question, with subordinate order:

> **ich weiß nicht mehr, welche Jacke ich anhatte**,
> *I don't remember which jacket I had on*

■ In older and literary German **welch** without any ending is the equivalent of **was für**:

> **welch eine (was für eine) Schande!**, *what a disgrace!*

▶ **Welcher** can stand alone without a noun as an interrogative pronoun (= *which one*, see p. 144) or as a relative pronoun (= *which* or *that*, see pp. 139–40).

INDEFINITE ADJECTIVES

Indefinite adjectives, as a group, include in English such words as *several, such, each, every*. In German almost all of them can be used both as adjectives and as pronouns and so they are more conveniently grouped together. A complete alphabetical list of all common indefinites, with both their adjective and their pronoun uses, can be found on pp. 144–58.

I Adverbs

Adverbs describe or modify a verb:

> **sie singt schön**, *she sings beautifully*

or an adjective:

> **sie hat eine unwahrscheinlich schöne Stimme**,
> *she has an incredibly beautiful voice*

or another adverb:

> **sie singt unwahrscheinlich schön**, *she sings
> incredibly beautifully*

or very occasionally a preposition or a conjunction:

> **oben im Apfelbaum**, *up in the apple tree*
> **mitten in der Rede**, *in the middle of the speech*
> **selbst wenn er das getan hat . . .** , *even if he's
> done that . . .*

ADVERB FORMATION

Most adjectives in German can be used unchanged, with no
endings, as adverbs. Quite a few adverbs exist only as adverbs,
however (**völlig**, *completely*; **unten**, *downstairs*; **außerdem**,
besides, etc.).

Adverbs ending -weise

Many adverbs are formed from a noun (or occasionally an
adjective + **-er**) + **weise**. For example:

from nouns:

> **teilweise**, *partly*
> **zeitweise**, *temporarily*
> **beispielsweise**, *for example*
> **ausnahmsweise**, *as an exception*

from adjectives:

> **glücklicherweise**, *luckily*
> **komischerweise**, *funnily enough*

A few of them may also be used as adjectives:

> **eine teilweise Senkung**, *a partial reduction*

Gern

The adverb **gern**, *gladly*, may be used with verbs to mean '*like*':

> **ich hab' dich gern**, *I like you*
> **ich esse gern Blumenkohl**, *I like cauliflower*
> **ich bin gern in Berlin**, *I like (being in) Berlin*

With **gern haben**, **gern** goes to the end of the sentence; in the expression **ich hätte gern**, *I should like*, **gern** always follows the verb; otherwise it stands in the normal position for a 'manner' adverb. See Word Order, p. 221.

Gern may have an **-e**, **gerne**, especially when standing alone:

> **kommst du mit? — Ja, gerne**, *are you coming along?—Yes, with pleasure*

▶ **Gern** has an irregular comparative and superlative: see p. 121.

Hier and da

These two adverbs can only be used to mean *here* and *there* when no motion is involved. When motion is involved **hierher** and **dahin** must be used:

> **sie steht da**, *she's standing there*
> **sie geht dahin**, *she's going there*

> **er bleibt hier**, *he's staying here*
> **er kommt hierher**, *he's coming here*

The **hin** or **her** can split off like a separable prefix:

> **da geht sie wieder hin**, *she's off there again*

The above also applies to **dort/dorthin**, *(to) there* (a more precisely localized place than **da**) and the question adverb **wo/wohin**, *(to) where*:

> **wo bist du?**, *where are you?*
> **wohin gehst du? / wo gehst du hin?**, *where are you going (to)?*

A similar use of **hin** for motion (though without the possibility of splitting off) is found with:

> **irgendwo/irgendwohin**, *somewhere or other*
> **überall/überallhin**, *everywhere*

Woher, *from where*, **irgendwoher**, *from somewhere or other*, and **überallher**, *from everywhere*, do not present a problem, since the *from* is obligatory in English.

COMPARATIVE AND SUPERLATIVE OF ADVERBS

Adverbs, like adjectives, form their comparative with the ending **-er** and their superlative with **-(e)st**.

■ Example: **leicht**, *easily*

□ Comparative: **leichter**

> **es läßt sich leichter machen**, *it can be done more easily*

□ Superlative: **am leichtesten**

das läßt sich am leichtesten machen, *that can be done most easily*

The extra **e** in the superlative is used (as above) where the word would be difficult or impossible to pronounce without it.

The superlative adverb form is identical with that of the adjective when standing alone. See p. 112.

■ Adjectives that modify their vowel in the comparative and superlative also modify when used as adverbs. See list, p. 112.

Oft, *often*, also modifies (**öfter, am öftesten**), though **häufiger**, *more frequently*, and **am häufigsten**, *most frequently*, tend to be used instead.

■ The following adverbs have irregular comparatives and superlatives:

	comparative	superlative
bald, *soon*	eher	am ehesten
gern, *gladly*	lieber	am liebsten

▶ For adjectives with irregular comparatives and superlatives (most of which can also be used as adverbs), see p. 113.

■ A group of superlative adverbs ending **-stens** correspond (generally) to the English *at (the)* + superlative. The commonest are:

frühstens, *at the earliest*	**nächstens**, *soon*
höchstens, *at most*	**spätestens**, *at the latest*
letztens, *recently*	**strengstens**, *most strictly*
meistens, *mostly*	**wärmstens**, *most warmly*
mindestens, *at least*	**wenigstens**, *at least*

The common spoken form **zumindestens**, *at least*, is a mixture of **mindestens**, included above, and the adverb **zumindest**, *at least*.

▶ For **erstens**, *firstly*, etc., see Numbers, p. 206.

■ *Than* after a comparative adverb is **als**, *as* after an expression of equality is **wie**:

er macht es leichter als ich, *he does it more easily than I (do)*

er macht es genau so leicht wie früher, *he does it just as easily as he used to*

This is similar to the constructions used with adjectives (see p. 114).

▶ For the order of adverbs and their position in the sentence, see Word Order, p. 221.

ALPHABETICAL LIST OF ADVERBIAL PARTICLES

Adverbial particles—words like **mal, doch, ja**—are much used, especially in spoken German, to give flavour to the language. There are English equivalents, but English relies more on differences of intonation and emphasis and uses particles much less freely. So they can rarely be translated directly from German into English. The following list gives the main adverbial particles with their basic meaning and examples of their use in various related meanings.

aber, *but*

■ adds emphasis

das war aber ausgezeichnet, *that was really outstanding*

du hast es schon wieder verloren? — Aber nein!, *you've lost it again?—No, of course I haven't*

allerdings, *admittedly*

■ *however, though* (concedes)

ihr Auto will ich kaufen, allerdings muß der Preis vernünftiger sein, *I intend to buy her car, though the price will have to be more reasonable*

■ agrees strongly with what is seen as obvious

> **es wird schwer sein — Ja, allerdings,** *it'll be hard—Well yes, of course*

Freilich is used with the same meaning in both instances. **Zwar** (see also p. 131) can be used with the first meaning above.

auch, *also*

■ *even*

> **auch du würdest es tun können,** *even you would be able to do it*
> **auch nicht meine Mutter würde so was sagen,** *even my mother wouldn't say something like that*
> **auch wenn er schreibt, werde ich kein Wort sagen,** *even if he writes I won't say a word*

■ *either* (with a negative)

> **sie macht es auch nicht,** *she won't do it either*
> **ich auch nicht,** *me neither*

■ correcting something that should have been obvious

> **das hat er auch nicht gesagt,** *but that's not what he said*

■ concessive *-ever*, with **wer, was, wie, wann** (producing *whoever, whatever, however, whenever*)

> **wie groß es auch sein mag, werden wir es gern liefern,** *however large it may be we'll gladly deliver it*

Note the position of **auch.**

■ emphasis

> **das mußt du auch tun,** *you really will have to do that, too*

denn, *then*

■ *then* (the English concessive *then*)

>   **gehst du denn?**, *are you going, then?*

Then = if that's the case is **dann**:

>   **dann gehe ich!**, *then (in that case) I'm going*

So is *then = at that point in time* or *next*:

>   **sie ging dann**, *then she went*

In north Germany **denn** is often—confusingly—misused for **dann**.

■ in **es sei denn, daß**, *unless*, and **geschweige denn**, *much less, let alone*

>   **ich hole ihn vom Bahnhof ab, es sei denn, daß
>   mein Auto wieder kaputt ist**, *I'll fetch him from
>   the station, unless my car's broken down again*
>   **radfahren kann sie nicht, geschweige denn
>   reiten**, *she can't ride a bike, let alone a horse*

doch, *yet*

■ *none the less, even so*

>   **wir haben ihn gewarnt, aber er ist doch darauf
>   getreten**, *we warned him, but he stepped on it just
>   the same*

Doch has stress in this use.

■ in a statement with question intonation, = **nicht wahr**

>   **du fliegst doch heute morgen?**, *your plane goes
>   this morning, doesn't it?*

■ *surely* (with a negative)

>   **du fliegst doch nicht mit dieser Luftlinie?**, *you're
>   surely not flying with that airline?*

■ *oh yes* (contradicting a negative statement or question, = French *si*)

> **du fliegst nicht heute — Doch!**, *you're not flying today—Oh yes I am*

It is sometimes strengthened with **ja** in this use: **ja doch!**

■ with the imperative, = *come on (now)*

> **sei doch vernünftig!**, *come on, be reasonable*

■ with **mal**, conveys encouragement

> **tu's doch mal!**, *go on, do it!*

eben, *just*

■ *just now*

> **sie ist eben angekommen**, *she has just arrived*

Gerade can be used with the same meaning; **soeben** is stronger, = *this very minute*.

■ *just = exactly*

> **eben das meinte ich**, *that's just (exactly) what I meant*
> **ja, eben**, *yes, exactly*

This is also the meaning of **eben-** in compounds: **ebensoviel**, *just as much; exactly that much*.

■ expressing resignation

> **dann eben nicht**, *well then, we won't*
> **das ist eben kalter Kaffee**, *that's just water under the bridge then*

In south Germany **halt** is used in this sense.

eigentlich, *really*

■ *in point of fact*

**es ist eigentlich viel schwerer als ich gedacht
habe**, *really (in fact) it's much harder than I thought*

The strengthening '*really*' is **wirklich**:

es ist wirklich schwer!, *it's <u>really</u> difficult!*

Similarly, as adjectives **wirklich** means *real = true*,
eigentlich means *real = fundamental*:

der wirkliche Unterschied, *the real (true) difference*
der eigentliche Unterschied, *the real difference (the
actual difference, in point of fact)*

einmal, *once*

▶ See **mal**, pp. 127–83.

etwa, *about*

■ *approximately*

etwa zehn Sekunden, *approximately ten seconds*

■ *by any chance, really*

hast du etwa Geld?, *do you have money, by any
chance?*
bist du etwa müde?, *are you perhaps tired?*
du willst doch nicht etwa sagen, daß . . . , *you
don't really mean to say that . . .*

Don't confuse with **etwas**, *some, somewhat*:

hast du etwas Geld?, *have you some money?*
du bist etwas müde, *you're a bit tired*

freilich, *admittedly*

▶ See **allerdings**, pp. 122–3.

gerade, *just*

▶ See **eben**, p. 125.

ja, *certainly*

■ *of course*

> **du wirst ihn ja kennen**, *you'll know him of course*
>
> **das weißt du ja schon**, *of course, you know that already*

■ underlining a fact, = *why!* or *really*

> **du bist ja schon da!**, *why, you're here already!*
>
> **das ist ja blöd**, *that really is stupid*
>
> **es ist ja direkt unglaublich**, *it's actually totally incredible*

■ concessive *of course*

> **sie ist ja furchtbar nett, aber . . .** , *she's awfully nice, of course, but . . .*

■ *indeed* (= *nay*)

> **er ist wohlhabend, ja sogar reich**, *he's well off, indeed you could even say (nay) rich*

mal; einmal, *once*

Mal is the more common in the spoken language in almost all cases. If **einmal** means literally *once* (i.e. *not twice*), the stress moves to the first syllable.

■ *one day, some day, sometime or other*

> **ich werde Sie (ein)mal in Deutschland besuchen**, *I'll visit you in Germany one day*
>
> **es war einmal ein Riese**, *once upon a time there was a giant*
>
> **irgend einmal**, *some time or other*

■ *for once*

> **ich will mal einen Kaffee trinken**, *I'll have a coffee for once*
>
> **(ein)mal zur Abwechslung**, *just once for a change*

■ with an exclamation or after **wollen**, = *just*

> **sei du (ein)mal ruhig!**, *you just be quiet!*
>
> **Augenblick mal!**, *just a moment*
>
> **laß mal sehen!**, *let's (just) have a look*
>
> **wir wollen mal sehen**, *we'll just have a look*

■ with **noch**, = *again*

> **tu's noch (ein)mal**, *do it again*

Noch (ein)mal implies the repetition of a specific action; **wieder**, *again*, is more general

> **sie ist wieder da**, *she's back again*

■ **nun (ein)mal** expresses resigned acceptance

> **die Sache ist nun (ein)mal so**, *that's the way things are*

noch, *yet*

■ *still, yet* (time)

> **bist du noch da?**, *are you still here?*
>
> **er ist noch nicht dreizehn**, *he's not yet thirteen*

Immer is used to strengthen **noch**, before it (**immer noch**) or after (**noch immer**).

■ *left*

> **wieviel Geld hast du noch?**, *how much money have you left?*

■ *more, further*

> **noch zwei Glas Wein, bitte**, *two more glasses of wine, please*

noch kleiner, *even smaller*
was noch?, *what else?*

nur, *only*

■ *only*

man kann nur lachen, *you can only (you've got to) laugh*
nur einmal, *only once*

■ *just (especially after exclamations)*

nur langsam!, *just do it slowly*
sehen Sie nur!, *just look!*
wenn ich nur bitten darf, *if I may just ask*

schon, *already*

■ *already, yet*

sie ist schon da, *she's already there*
ist sie schon dagewesen?, *has she been there yet?*

■ *as early as*

er wird schon morgen hier sein, *he'll be here as early as tomorrow*

■ *even*

schon das war zuviel, *even that was too much*

■ *certainly, I'm sure*

er wird schon kommen, *he'll certainly come*
das stimmt schon, *I'm sure that's true*
ich glaube schon, *I think so*

■ *with weil and wegen, = if only because*

ich darf nicht mitkommen, schon weil es so spät anfängt, *I can't come with you, if only because it begins so late*

weiter, *further*

■ *further*

> **das Haus liegt etwas weiter entfernt**, *the house is a bit further away*

■ *else*, when **weiter** is used with **nichts** or in a question

> **und weiter nichts**, *and nothing else (nothing further)*
> **was ist weiter zu tun?**, *what else is there to do?*

Sonst is an alternative to **weiter** in this meaning.

■ *on*

> **sprich mal weiter**, *just go on speaking*

■ **weiter nicht** = *not that*

> **das ist weiter nicht schlimm**, *that doesn't matter very much (that's not that bad)*

wirklich, *really*

▶ See **eigentlich**, pp. 125–6.

wohl, *indeed*

■ *indeed, certainly*

> **das kann man wohl sagen**, *you can certainly say that*

The **wohl** is moderately stressed.

■ *probably*

> **sie wird wohl jetzt zu Hause sein**, *she's probably home by now*

The **wohl** is not stressed.

■ *full well*

> **das weißt du wohl**, *you know very well*

The **wohl** is moderately stressed.

■ *admittedly*

> **ich war wohl dafür verantwortlich, habe aber
> trotzdem nichts getan,** *I was indeed responsible
> for it, but in spite of that I did nothing*

The **wohl** is moderately stressed.

■ **wohl aber** = *but on the other hand*

> **ich kenne ihn nicht, wohl aber seinen Bruder,**
> *I don't know him, but I do know his brother*

The **wohl** is strongly stressed.

zwar, *admittedly*

■ *admittedly*

> **der ist zwar langsam, aber nicht faul,** *admittedly
> he's slow, but not lazy*

▶ For this meaning see also **allerdings**, pp. 122–3.

■ **und zwar** = *and furthermore* (introduces an extra phrase to
clarify or extend)

> **er kommt immer früh an, und zwar gegen
> sieben,** *he always arrives early—about seven in fact*

I Pronouns

PERSONAL PRONOUNS

The basic use of the four cases of personal pronouns is similar to that of nouns. See p. 96.

Forms of the personal pronouns

The subject (nominative) pronouns are:

singular	*plural*
ich, *I*	**wir**, *we*
du, *you*	**ihr**, *you*
Sie, *you* (polite form)	
er, *he*; **sie**, *she*; **es**, *it*	**sie**, *they*

The direct object (accusative) pronouns are:

singular	*plural*
mich, *me*	**uns**, *us*
dich, *you*	**euch**, *you*
Sie, *you* (polite form)	
ihn, *him*; **sie**, *her*; **es**, *it*	**sie**, *them*

The indirect object (dative) pronouns are:

singular	*plural*
mir, *to me*	**uns**, *to us*
dir, *to you*	**euch**, *to you*
Ihnen, *to you* (polite form)	
ihm, *to him/to it*; **ihr**, *to her*	**ihnen**, *to them*

The reflexive pronouns are:

singular	*plural*
mich (accusative), *myself*;	**uns**, *(to) ourselves*
mir (dative), *to myself*	

dich (accusative), *yourself*;   **euch**, *(to)* yourselves
dir (dative), *to yourself*
sich, *(to) yourself/-selves* (polite form)
sich, *(to) him-/her-/itself*   **sich**, *(to) themselves*

■ The polite pronoun **Sie**, *you*, is both singular and plural. It always has a capital in all forms except the reflexive **sich**. In letter-writing **du** and **ihr** are also written with a capital, in all their forms (including the possessives **dein**, **euer**).

■ The familiar forms **du** and **ihr** are used to friends, relatives, colleagues, children, and animals. The plural form **ihr** is used both for more than one '**du**' and for a mixed group of **du**'s and **Sie**'s. God is addressed as **Du** with a capital. Teachers use **Sie** to students in the last three forms of the Gymnasium, equivalent to the English sixth form. Using **du** to someone one is on **Sie** terms with, without their permission, is rude.

wollen wir uns duzen?, *shall we start using 'du' to each other?*

■ Pronouns agree in gender with the noun they refer to:

wo ist mein Bleistift? — ah, ich hab' ihn, *where's my pencil?—ah, I've got it*

However, **sie** is usually used to refer to **(das) Mädchen**, *girl*, and **(das) Fräulein**, *girl, Miss*.

■ The indefinite pronoun **man**, *one*, has the accusative and dative forms **einen** and **einem**. Its reflexive form is **sich**, its possessive **sein**. See pp. 153–4.

■ Genitive of the personal pronoun (*of me*, etc.).

The forms are:

meiner, *of me*; **deiner**, *of you*; **seiner**, *of him, of it*;
ihrer, *of her, of them*; **unser**, *of us*; **euer**, *of you*

They sound literary and are usually avoided as follows:

☐ Prepositions that take the genitive may be used with the dative instead.

☐ Verbs that can take the genitive (e.g. **sich erinnern**) always have a preferable alternative construction (e.g. **sich erinnern an** + accusative).

☐ Adjectives that take the genitive use **dessen**, *of that*, instead of **seiner**, and **derselben**, *of the same*, instead of **ihrer**.

Virtually the only time the genitive personal pronoun is used in modern German is with the adjectives **sicher**, *sure*, and **würdig**, *worthy*, which take a preceding genitive and have no alternative construction:

> **bist du seiner ganz sicher?**, *are you quite sure of him?*

Es as anticipatory object

A number of verbs insert the pronoun **es** as an anticipatory object into their main clause when they have a clause beginning **daß**, or an infinitive phrase, as their real object:

> **ich kann es nicht ertragen, daß er immer so spät kommt**, *I can't stand him always coming so late*
> **sie hat es fertiggebracht, ihr Visum zu bekommen**, *she has managed to get her visa*

This is obligatory with the following verbs:

ablehnen, to refuse	**genießen**, to enjoy
aushalten, to endure	**lassen**, to refrain from
erreichen, to manage	**lieben**, to love
ertragen, to endure	**unterlassen**, to omit
fertigbringen, to manage	**verstehen**, to know how to

Es is also always used with expressions such as **es eilig haben**, *to be in a hurry*, **es satt haben**, *to be sick of*, **es nötig haben**, *to need*, where the **es** forms part of the verbal phrase:

ich habe es eilig, *I'm in a hurry*

ich habe es eilig, nach Hause zu kommen, *I'm in a hurry to get home*

In addition to the list above there are many other verbs with which an anticipatory **es** may occasionally be found.

Reflexive pronouns

These are used where the direct or indirect object of the verb is the same as the subject. In addition:

■ In German a reflexive pronoun is used after a preposition to refer back to the subject of the sentence:

diese Zeit hat sie jetzt hinter sich, *she's got those days behind her now*

sie hatte nur zehn Mark bei sich, *she only had ten marks with her*

■ A dative reflexive is used in the phrase **vor sich hin**, *to oneself*, usually with a verb of speaking:

er redete vor sich hin, *he was talking to himself*

▶ See also Reflexive Verbs, p. 27.

POSSESSIVE PRONOUNS

In German there are several forms of the possessive pronoun (in English: *mine, yours, hers*, etc.). The most common form is **meiner** (etc.), declined like **dieser**:

	masculine	*feminine*	*neuter*	*plural*
nominative	meiner, *mine*	meine	mein(e)s	meine
accusative	meinen	meine	mein(e)s	meine
genitive	meines	meiner	meines	meiner
dative	meinem	meiner	meinem	meinen

The forms corresponding to **meiner** for the other persons are:

deiner, etc., *yours*
Ihrer, etc., *yours* (polite form)
seiner, etc., *his; its own*
uns(e)rer, etc., *ours*
eu(e)rer, etc., *yours*
ihrer, etc., *hers; theirs*

■ In the neuter nominative and accusative the **-e** is usually dropped in **meins, deins, seins, ihrs, Ihrs.**

■ **Eu(e)rer** (usually) and **uns(e)rer** (sometimes) lose the final **e** of their stem when they have an ending:

> **eure sind besser als uns(e)re**, *yours are better than ours*

■ The following forms are also found:

□   **mein**, *mine*
       dein, *yours*
       sein, *his; its own*
       unser, *ours*
       euer, *yours*

These take no endings, are formal or poetic, and can only be used after the verb **sein:**

> **mein Herz ist dein**, *my heart is yours*

They are never used after **es/das ist**. Furthermore, '**ihr**', *hers/theirs*, and '**Ihr**', *yours* (polite form) don't exist.

□   **der meine, die meine, das meine**, *mine*
       der deine, die deine, das deine, *yours*
       etc.

In this form of the possessive pronoun **mein-** etc. is treated as an adjective after the definite article. It is rather less common than the first form given above (**meiner** etc.), especially in spoken German.

□ The form **der meinige, der deinige**, etc., where **meinig-** etc. is also an adjective, is also found. It sounds a little old-fashioned.

■ The English genitive form *of mine* (etc.) is **von mir** (etc.):

> **die sind Bekannte von mir**, *they're acquaintances of mine*

DEMONSTRATIVE PRONOUNS

Demonstrative pronouns single out ('demonstrate') particular people or things. The demonstrative pronouns in German are **dieser**, *this (one)*, **der** or **jener**, *that (one)*, **derjenige**, *the one*, and **wer**, *the one who*. **Dieser** and **jener** are identical in form with the demonstrative adjectives **dieser** and **jener** (see p. 86).

Dieser, jener, der

Except in the special meaning of *the former*, **jener** has dropped out of common use. **Dieser** may be used for both *this one* and *that one*:

> **geben Sie mir dieses, bitte**, *give me that (this), please*

Frequently **der**, emphasized in speech and sometimes followed by **da**, *there*, is used for *that one* (plural: *those*):

> **stellen sie es zu denen (da), bitte**, *put it with those, please*

As a demonstrative pronoun **der** is declined like the relative pronoun **der** (see p. 139). **Dieser** and **jener** are declined like the definite article **der** (see p. 86).

The form **dies** is often found, especially in conversation, instead of **dieses** (neuter nominative and accusative):

> **dies ist aber wunderschön**, *this one is really marvellous*

■ For *this one*, *that one* after a preposition the compounds with **da(r)-** are used:

legen Sie es bitte darunter, *put it under that (one),
please*

In this use, where **da-** = *this one/that one*, the stress in spoken
German goes on the 'da'. Compare **da-** = *it*, p. 162.

■ The demonstrative spoken without stress is often used in
conversation instead of **er**, *he*, **sie**, *she/they*, and **es**, *it*. It is
particularly useful to distinguish **sie**, *they*, from **Sie**, *you*:

die sind wirklich häßlich, *they're really ugly* (**sie**
would be ambiguous in speech!)

The neuter forms **das** and (less common) **dies**, unstressed,
are alternatives to **es** used with **sein**, *to be*, postponing the real
subject; they are used with both a singular and a plural verb:

**das (dies) ist meine Mutter, und das (dies) sind
meine Schwestern**, *that's my mother and those
are my sisters*

■ **Dieser** and **jener** also mean, respectively, *the latter* and *the
former*. They are used in these meanings without the rather
literary sound that 'the latter' and 'the former' have in English:

**was Hans und seinen Bruder betrifft: dieser ist
schon bei der Bundeswehr gewesen, jener hat
seinen Militärdienst noch nicht abgeleistet**, *as far
as Hans and his brother are concerned, the latter has
(Hans's brother has) been in the army, the former has
(Hans has) not yet done his national service*

Derjenige

The demonstrative pronoun **derjenige** (fem.: **diejenige**, neut.:
dasjenige) means *the one*. Both parts of the word decline, the
second part as an adjective after the definite article. **Derjenige**
is usually followed by the relative **der**:

ich suche denjenigen, den er mitgebracht hat,
I'm looking for the one he brought with him

Derjenige is literary; in conversation the demonstrative **der** is used instead:

> **ich suche den, den er mitgebracht hat**

Wer

Wer is the equivalent of 'derjenige, der'. It refers to people and has the general meaning of *anybody who, those who, the one who*. It always stands at the head of the sentence.

> **wer schon bezahlt hat, darf daran teilnehmen,**
> *anyone who has already paid may take part*

Distinguish **wer** followed by subordinate order, meaning *anybody who*, from **wer** introducing a question, meaning *who?*:

> **wer hat schon bezahlt?**, *who's already paid?*

RELATIVE PRONOUNS

Relative pronouns introduce a subordinate clause within the sentence and usually relate it back to a noun in the main clause. In English they are *who, whom, whose, which, that, what*.

The relative pronouns in German are **der** and **welcher**, which are identical in meaning and can refer to either people (*who*, etc.; *that*) or things (*which*; *that*). They introduce subordinate order, sending the verb to the end of the clause.

There is a third relative, **was** (*what*), which introduces a noun clause (see pp. 141–2). **Was** is invariable; the forms of **der** and **welcher** are as follows:

der

	masculine	*feminine*	*neuter*	*plural*
nominative	der	die	das	die
accusative	den	die	das	die
genitive	dessen	deren	dessen	deren
dative	dem	der	dem	denen

welcher

	masculine	feminine	neuter	plural
nominative	welcher	welche	welches	welche
accusative	welchen	welche	welches	welche
dative	welchem	welcher	welchem	welchen

☐ **Welcher** has no genitive forms and is less frequently used than **der**. For **welcher** as an interrogative adjective introducing a subordinate clause, see p. 117.

☐ **Welcher** can't be used after indefinite pronouns referring to people (**niemand**, *nobody*, **jemand**, *somebody*, etc.):

> **kennen Sie jemand, der das tun könnte?**, *do you know anybody who could do that?*

☐ Beware! Distinguish carefully the relative **das**, *that*, referring back to a neuter noun, from the conjunction **daß**, *that*, introducing a clause and not referring back to any noun.

☐ Relatives can be omitted in English: *the man (that) you're speaking to*, but not in German.

■ Relatives agree in gender and number with the noun or pronoun they refer back to; but their case depends on their function in the clause they introduce. So:

> **der Mann, den Sie eingestellt haben, ist ein alter Freund von mir**, *the man that you have appointed is an old friend of mine*

Den is singular and masculine, because **der Mann**, to which it refers back, is singular and masculine. **Den** is accusative, however, because in the clause it introduces it is the object of **eingestellt haben**.

☐ Exactly the same rule applies to the genitive relative:

> **der Mann, dessen Tochter Sie eingestellt haben, ist ein alter Freund von mir**, *the man whose daughter you have appointed is an old friend of mine*

Dessen is masculine because **Mann** is masculine (and in spite of the fact that it stands before the feminine word **Tochter**).

☐ Where a thing rather than a person is referred to with a genitive, English often uses *of which* after the noun. German still uses **dessen/deren** and does not change the normal word order:

> **dieses Buch, dessen Anfang Sie vorgelesen haben**, *that book, the beginning of which (whose beginning) you read out*

■ A relative may follow a preposition. It stands in the case that normally follows that preposition:

> **der Herr, mit dem du sprichst . . .** , *the man you're speaking to* (literally, *with whom you're speaking*)
>
> **der Herr, mit dessen Frau du sprichst . . .** , *the man whose wife you're speaking to* (literally, *with whose wife you're speaking*)

In English the preposition may stand either in front of the relative (*to whose wife you're speaking*), or, less clumsily, at the end of the clause (*whose wife you're speaking to*). Only the first of these two is possible in German.

☐ A less common alternative to preposition plus relative is a compound formed with **wo-** plus the preposition: **von dem→wovon**. This form can only be used to refer to things. Before a preposition beginning with a vowel an **r** is inserted: **auf dem→worauf**.

> **der Stuhl, worauf du sitzt, gehörte meinen Großeltern**, *the chair you're sitting on belonged to my grandparents*

In conversation **auf dem** would be more likely.

■ **Was** is used

☐ (= *which*) to refer back to a clause:

er ist gewählt worden, was ich kaum glauben kann, *he has been elected, which (something) I can hardly believe*

☐ (= *what*) at the beginning of the sentence, to introduce a noun clause:

was ich kaum glauben kann, ist die Tatsache, daß . . . , *what I can scarcely believe, is the fact that . . .*

☐ (= *that*; *which*) as the relative after the indefinite pronouns **alles**, *everything*, **nichts**, *nothing*, **das**, *that*, **vieles**, *much*, **weniges**, *little*, and usually after **etwas**, *something*, and **folgendes**, *the following*:

fast alles, was er sagt, ist Unsinn, *nearly everything (that) he says is nonsense*

☐ (= *that*) as the relative after neuter adjectival nouns:

das ist das Beste, was du je getan hast, *that's the best thing you've ever done*

Was is not used after a preposition; **wo(r)-** + preposition is substituted:

alles, woraus unsere Produkte hergestellt sind, *everything that our products are made from*

Was may of course introduce a question as well, either direct or indirect:

was meinst du?, *what do you mean?*
ich weiß nicht, was du meinst, *I don't know what you mean*

▶ For **wer** as combined demonstrative and relative (= *the one who*) see p. 139.

INTERROGATIVE PRONOUNS

The interrogative pronouns in English are *who?*, *what?*, and *which?* In German they are **wer?**, *who?*, **was?**, *what?*, and **welcher**, *which?*. **Wer** and **was** decline as follows:

nominative	wer?	was?
accusative	wen?	was?
genitive	wessen?	wessen?
dative	wem?	

They may be used in both direct and indirect questions:

> **wer sagt das?**, *who says so?*
>
> **ich weiß nicht, was er gesagt hat**, *I don't know what he said*
>
> **wessen Kugelschreiber hast du da?**, *whose pen have you got there?*
>
> **ich weiß nicht, wem er gehört**, *I don't know who it belongs to*

■ **Was** has no dative and its genitive is little used.

■ Both **wer** and **was** have no plural forms, though they may have a plural meaning, and with the verb **sein** they may take a plural verb form:

> **wer sind diese Dummköpfe?**, *who are these idiots?*

With other verbs this is impossible: **alles** is added instead where a plural has to be indicated:

> **wer kommt denn alles?**, *who is/are coming then?*

■ After a preposition **was** is not normally used, especially in written German; **wo(r)-** + preposition is substituted:

> **womit schreibst du?**, *what are you writing with?*

The extra **-r** is used before a preposition beginning with a vowel.

The compounds **wohin** and **woher** are used to ask about motion towards and away from:

wohin gehst du?, *where are you going (to)?*
woher kommst du?, *where have you come from?*

NB: with **durch**: **wodurch** = *by what means*, **durch was** = *through what* (motion).

■ *Which (one)?* is **welcher?**, used as a pronoun:

hol mir meinen Mantel! — Welchen?, *get me my coat—Which one?*

▶ *Which* can also be an interrogative adjective (*which book?*). In this case it is **welcher**. See pp. 116–7.

ALPHABETICAL LIST OF INDEFINITE PRONOUNS AND ADJECTIVES

Indefinite pronouns (*somebody, something, anybody*, etc. in English) all take the third person (**er** form) of the verb in German, as they do in English. The forms of object pronouns, reflexives, possessives corresponding to the indefinite pronouns are also third-person masculine forms (**ihn, sich, sein**, and their plurals).

jeder erinnert sich an seine Vergangenheit,
everyone remembers his (their) past

Indefinites all have a small letter in German. Some indefinites only function as pronouns, most can also be used as adjectives.

The genitive forms of the indefinites are in most cases rare, problematic, or unused. They are best avoided (use **von** or rephrase the sentence) except in the specific cases mentioned below.

The alphabetical list includes all common indefinite pronouns and adjectives.

■ **alles**, *everything; anything;* **alle**, *all; everybody;* **sämtlich**, *all; complete*

□ **Alles** and **alle** decline like **dieses** and **diese** (see p. 86). As in English, **alle**, *all*, can either itself be the subject of the sentence, or stand after the verb with a personal pronoun as subject:

> **alles ist möglich**, *everything is possible*
> **alle waren da / sie waren alle da**, *they were all there*
> **alle vier waren da / sie waren alle vier da**, *all four were there*

In the spoken language the neuter singular **alles** is used to mean *nothing but* or *entirely:*

> **das waren alles Parteimitglieder**, *they were every one of them party members*

and, also in the spoken language, **alle** is used as an adjective to mean '*all gone':*

> **das Bier ist alle**, *we've run out of beer*

□ As an adjective (*all*), **all** takes no endings and stands in front of the article (or possessive or demonstrative):

> **all die Soldaten**, *all (of) the soldiers*
> **trotz all deines Geldes**, *in spite of all your money*

If there is no article (or possessive or demonstrative) following, it declines like **dieser:**

> **alle Leute wissen das — alle intelligenten Leute**, *everybody knows that—all intelligent people*

□ The adjective **sämtlich** means *complete:*

> **Shakespeares sämtliche Werke**, *Shakespeare's complete works*

It is also very commonly used to mean *all* as an adjective, especially in the plural:

die sämtlichen Soldaten, *all the soldiers*
dein sämtliches Geld, *all your money*

Preceded by an article (or a possessive or demonstrative adjective) **sämtlich** behaves as an adjective; otherwise an adjective after it takes **-en**:

sämtliche intelligenten Leute, *all intelligent people*

□ Note that **ganz** can also translate *all* where it means *whole*:

die ganze Zeit, *all the time* (= *the whole time*)

■ **ander**, *other*, **ein and(e)rer**, *somebody else*, **der and(e)re**, *the other one*

Ander declines as an adjective; when it has an ending it often drops the **e** of the stem:

ein andrer wüßte das nicht, *anybody else wouldn't know that*
alles andere, *everything else*

It often follows numbers rather than standing in front of them:

die zwei anderen Kinder, *the other two children* (**die anderen zwei** is possible, however)

Where *other* means *more* it is **noch**:

eine andere Flasche Wein, *another bottle of wine* (a different one—there's something wrong with this one)
noch eine Flasche Wein, *another bottle of wine* (a further one—we've finished this one)

■ **anders**, *different(ly)*; *else*

□ **Anders** is invariable and is used after **sein** or as an adverb:

die Sache ist ganz anders, *the matter is quite different*
das mußt du anders machen, *you'll have to do that differently*

In front of a noun *different* is **ander-**:

eine andere Sache, *a different matter*

☐ **Anders** is also used to mean *else* after **jemand** and **niemand**, **wer** and **wo**. It is invariable; in the case of **wo** it often joins up:

das war niemand anders als sein Onkel, *it was no one else but (none other than) his uncle*

wo kann es anders sein?, *where else can it be?*

es muß woanders sein, *it must be somewhere else*

■ **beide**, *both; two*

☐ **Beide** declines like **dieser** (see p. 86) when it stands alone:

sie sind beide da / beide sind da, *they are both there*

After a definite article it declines as an adjective. Note the different word order: *both the* is **die beiden**:

die beiden Studenten, *both the students; the two students*

Die beiden is a very common alternative to **die zwei** for *the two*. **Beide** is the normal word used with personal pronouns:

wir beide, *the two of us*

Einer von beiden means *one or other (of them)*; **keiner von beiden** means *neither of them*:

keiner von beiden will es tun, *neither of them wants to do it*

Beide may be strengthened with **alle**: **alle beide**, *both of you, both of us*, etc.:

ihr seid alle beide eingeladen, *both of you are invited*

☐ **Beides** can also be used as a neuter (often as an alternative to **beide**)—it is singular and invariable and is found in places where in English a plural would be used. It takes a singular verb except when used with **sein** and a plural noun:

> **ich habe beides gesehen**, *I've seen both (of them)*
>
> **beides wäre möglich**, *both (either) would be possible*
>
> **es waren beides Parteimitglieder / beides waren Parteimitglieder**, *they were both party members* (compare **alles**, p. 145)

■ **ein**, *one*; **einer**, *one*; **someone**

□ As well as being the indefinite article (see p. 87), **ein** can be a pronoun, when it declines like **dieses** (see p. 86). Its masculine form **einer** is used to refer to people when gender is not specified:

> **einer von uns muß es tun**, *one of us must do it*
>
> **einer muß es tun**, *someone must do it*

The **e** of the nominative and accusative **eines** is often dropped:

> **eins von beiden**, *one of the two*

Ein(e)s often means *one thing*:

> **eins muß ich sagen**, *there's one thing I've got to say*

▶ **Einen** and **einem** substitute for the non-existent accusative and dative of **man**. See p. 153.

□ **Ein**, *one*, can also be used as an adjective, when it takes adjective endings:

> **er kam in dem einen Auto an, fuhr in dem anderen ab**, *he arrived in (the) one car and left in the other*

□ The compounded form **unsereiner** means *the likes of us, people of our sort*. It declines like the pronoun **einer** and has no plural or genitive singular. The neuter **unsereins** is used in spoken German for either sex:

> **unsereins** (less colloquial: **unsereiner**) **fährt nicht erster Klasse**, *our sort don't go first class*

■ **ein bißchen**, *a bit; a little* (in south Germany almost always: **ein bissel**); **ein paar**, *a few*

Normally invariable:

> **er ist ein bißchen verrückt**, *he's a bit mad*
>
> **mit ein bißchen Geld kann man alles machen**,
> *with a bit of money you can do anything*
>
> **mit ein paar Leuten**, *with a few people*

but *the little bit* is **das bißchen**, *the few* is **die paar**, which change according to case:

> **mit dem bißchen Geld, das ich noch habe**, *with*
> *the little bit of money I still have*
>
> **mit den paar Leuten, die noch mit mir sprechen**,
> *with the few people who still speak to me*

The words **bißchen** and **paar** are always spelled with a small letter in these constructions.

▶ See also **einige**, *a few*, below, and **wenige**, *(very) few*, p. 158.

■ **einige**, *some, a few*

□ **Einige** is usually plural; it is declined like plural **diese** (see p. 86). It can be used as a pronoun or an adjective:

> **einige waren Deutsche**, *some (a few) were*
> *Germans*
>
> **einige Journalisten standen vorm Rathaus**, *a few*
> *journalists were standing in front of the town hall*

▶ **Einige** means *a few*; *the few* is **die wenigen** or **die paar** (see this page, above). *Few* (= *very few*) is **wenige**: see p. 158.

□ **Einige** is occasionally found in the singular: **einiger**, **einige**, **einiges**. It is used both as a pronoun and as an adjective:

> **einiges bleibt noch**, *some of it is still left*
>
> **vor einiger Zeit**, *some time ago*

■ **ein paar**, *a few*

▶ See **ein bißchen**, p. 149.

■ **etwas**, *something, anything; somewhat; some*; **nichts**, *nothing*

□ **Etwas** as a pronoun means *something* or *anything*:

> **ich muß dir etwas zeigen**, *I must show you something*

In conversation the pronoun **etwas** is very often shortened to **was**:

> **können Sie mir was zeigen?**, *can you show me anything?*

So etwas means *that sort of thing, something like that*:

> **haben Sie so etwas wie dieses, aber in Rot?**, *have you got something like this, only in red?*
>
> **nein, so was führen wir nicht**, *no, we don't keep that sort of thing*

So was is also used as an exclamation:

> **na, so was!**, *well, would you believe it!*

□ **Nichts** means *not . . . anything* as well as *nothing*:

> **ich kann Ihnen nichts zeigen**, *I can't show you anything*

Qualifying adverbs, e.g. **gar/durchaus**, *at all*, **sonst**, *else*, precede it:

> **hier ist gar nichts**, *there's nothing at all here*
>
> **ich habe sonst nichts**, *I've nothing else*

▶ **Nichts** and **(et)was** may be followed by a neuter adjective with a capital letter (**nichts Gutes**, *nothing good*): see p. 108.

□ **Etwas** can also be used adjectivally:

> **ich habe gerade etwas Zeit**, *I have some (a little) time at the moment*

and, often, as an adverb:

> **er ist etwas geizig**, *he's somewhat (a bit) mean*

■ **irgend etwas, irgend jemand, irgendein**, etc.

□ **Irgend** adds the sense of *'or other'* or *'at all'* to another indefinite: **irgend etwas**, *something or other, anything at all*; **irgend jemand**, *someone or other, anyone at all*:

> **hast du irgend etwas gesehen?**, *did you see anything (at all)?*
>
> **irgend jemand muß es getan haben**, *somebody or other (somebody) must have done it*

□ **Irgend** joins up with the following, forming adverbs:

> **wann: irgendwann**, *some time or other*
> **wie: irgendwie**, *somehow, anyhow*
> **wo: irgendwo**, *somewhere or other*
> **wohin: irgendwohin**, *(to) somewhere or other*
> **woher: irgendwoher**, *from somewhere or other*
>
> **wir werden uns irgendwann wiedersehen**, *we'll see each other again sometime (or other)*

□ **Irgend** joins up with **was = etwas**, forming a pronoun:

> **du mußt irgendwas tun**, *you must do something*

□ **Irgend** joins up with the following, forming adjectives:

> **ein: irgendein**, *some . . . or other*
> **welcher: irgendwelcher**, *some . . . or other*
>
> **das muß irgendeinen Sinn haben**, *that must have some (sort of) meaning*

Irgendein declines like **ein**, the indefinite article (see p. 87).

Irgendwelcher declines like **dieser** (see p. 86); it is mainly used before abstract nouns and as the plural of **irgendein** (**ein** has no plural):

> **habt ihr irgendwelche Schwierigkeiten damit gehabt?**, *did you have any difficulties with it?*

□ **Irgendeiner** and **irgendwelcher** are pronoun forms of **irgendein** and **irgendwelche**. They are declined like **dieser** (see p. 86) and mean *someone or other.*

> **irgendeiner wird da sein**, *someone or other will be there*

■ **jeder**, *everyone*; *every*, *each*, **jedermann**, *everyone*

□ **Jeder** is declined like **dieser**:

> **jeder weiß, wie groß es ist**, *everyone knows how big it is*

It is very frequently used as an adjective, declined in the same way:

> **jeder Zehnjährige weiß, wie groß es ist**, *every ten-year-old knows how big it is*

It is occasionally used in the plural:

> **jede zehn Sekunden**, *every ten seconds*

It can also be used after **ein**, to form **ein jeder**, *each and every one*. Here it behaves as an adjective after **ein**:

> **er begrüßte einen jeden persönlich**, *he greeted each and every one personally*

□ **Jedermann** is an alternative to **jeder**. It is much less common, can only be used as a pronoun, is singular, and takes an ending only in the genitive:

> **dieses Gericht ist nicht jedermanns Sache**, *this dish isn't to everyone's liking*

■ **jemand**, *somebody*; **niemand**, *nobody*

These decline as follows:

nominative	**jemand**	**niemand**
accusative	**jemand** or **jemanden**	**niemand** or **niemanden**
genitive	**(jemand(e)s)**	**(niemand(e)s)**
dative	**jemand** or **jemandem**	**niemand** or **niemandem**

Both forms of the accusative and dative are common in speech; the form with the ending is more usual in writing. The genitive is little used.

Somebody else, nobody else is **sonst jemand, sonst niemand**.

▶ For **jemand/niemand Schönes**, *someone/no one beautiful*, see Adjectives, p. 108.

▶ For **irgend jemand** see **irgend**, p. 151.

■ **keiner**, *no one*; **kein**, *no*

□ As a pronoun **keiner** declines like **dieser** (see p. 86). It is more precise than **niemand**, often being the equivalent of *none, not one*:

> **keiner weiß, wie er aussieht**, *no one knows what he looks like*

> **keiner von uns hat ihn gesehen**, *none of us (not a single one of us) has seen him*

□ As an adjective **kein** declines like **ein**: see p. 87. It is always used instead of **nicht ein** except
to stress the *one*:

> **nicht ein Pfennig Geld**, *not one penny, not a single penny*

when **nicht** and **ein** are split for stylistic emphasis:

> **einen Tiroler Hut hab' ich nicht!**, *I don't <u>possess</u> a Tyrolean hat*

after **wenn**:

> **ich hätte es nicht gesagt, wenn Sie nicht einen Tiroler Hut getragen hätten**, *I wouldn't have said it if you hadn't been wearing a Tyrolean hat*

before **sondern** ('*not this but that*'):

> **das ist nicht ein Tiroler Hut, sondern ein bayrischer**, *that's not a Tyrolean hat, it's Bavarian*

■ **man**, *one, we, you, they, people in general*

Man is a subject pronoun, taking the **er** form of the verb. It corresponds to the English *one*, but whereas spoken English

avoids *one* as formal (using *we, they, people* . . . instead),
German uses **man** quite informally, much as French uses *on*.

Man has the reflexive **sich** and the possessive **sein**; it has no
cases other than the nominative, borrowing **einen** for
accusative, **einem** for dative, and avoiding the genitive.

> **man sagt, daß . . .** , *people say that*
>
> **man kratzt sich nicht in der Öffentlichkeit**, *one
> does not scratch in public*
>
> **dort kann es einem zu warm werden**, *it can get
> too hot for you there*

The possessive **sein** cannot be used to refer to **man** as part
of the subject—the rather cumbersome '**das man hat**' has to
be used instead:

> **die Ideen, die man hat, sind oft am Anfang nicht
> ganz klar**, *one's ideas are often not entirely clear to
> start with*

■ **manche**, *many*; **mancher**, *many a*

□ **Manche** is plural; it is declined like plural **diese** (see p. 86).
It is often identical in meaning with **viele** (see pp. 156–7).
Manche . . . manche means *some (people) . . . some (people)*:

> **manche sagen ja, manche dagegen sagen nein**,
> *some say yes, some on the other hand say no*

The singular, **mancher**, *many a one*, is a little old-fashioned:

> **mancher wäre auch dieser Meinung**, *many a one
> (many people) would also be of this opinion*

□ **Mancher** is also used as an adjective, also declined like
dieser. An adjective following it behaves like an adjective
following **dieser**. **Mancher** quite often has a (meaningless) **so**
in front of it:

> **manche Frauen sind nicht deiner Meinung**, *many
> women wouldn't agree with you*
>
> **so mancher brave Mann**, *many an honest man*

Manch can be used without an ending before **ein**:

> **manch eine Frau**, *many a woman*

This too is rather old-fashioned.

■ **mehrere**, *several*

Mehrere is only found in the plural. It declines like an ordinary adjective, and a second adjective after it takes the same ending as **mehrere**:

> **mehrere ungewöhnliche Tatsachen**, *several unusual facts*

■ **nichts**, *nothing*

▶ See **etwas**, p. 150.

■ **niemand**, *no one*

▶ See **jemand**, p. 152.

■ **sämtlich**, *all*

▶ See **alles**, p. 145.

■ **solch**, *such*; **so ein**, *such a*

□ In the singular **solch** is most frequently used as an adjective. The word order is different from the English:

> **ein solcher Film zieht ein großes Publikum an**, *such a film attracts a large audience*

□ In conversation **so ein** is frequently substituted for **ein solcher**:

> **hast du je so einen Film gesehen?**, *have you ever seen a film like that?*

So is always used after **kein**:

> **das war kein so hervorragender Film**, *that wasn't such a terrific film*

□ **Solch ein** is also found, but is not common in speech:

solch ein hervorragender Film, *such an outstanding film*

In this construction **solch** is invariable.

☐ The pronoun form of **solch** is **solcher**, declined like **dieser** (see p. 86):

den Film als solchen fand ich nicht so hervorragend, *I didn't find the film as such so terrific*

This form is also used as an adjective in the plural (since the **ein** of **ein solcher** and **so ein** has no plural form):

solche Filme interessieren mich nicht, *such films (films like that) don't interest me*

It is occasionally used in the singular (**so** is commoner):

bei solchem schlechten Wetter bleibe ich zu Hause, *in such bad weather I stay at home*

▶ For **so etwas** see **etwas**, p. 150.

■ **unsereiner**, *people of our sort*

▶ See **einer**, p. 148.

■ **viel**, *much*; **viele**, *many*

☐ As a pronoun **viel** is declined:

	singular	*plural*
nominative	**viel** or **vieles**	**viele**
accusative	**viel** or **vieles**	**viele**
genitive		**vieler**
dative	**viel** or **vielem**	**vielen**

nicht viele denken wie du, *not many think like you*
viel(es), was du sagst, ist unverständlich, *much that (of what) you say is incomprehensible*

The form without an ending is sometimes said to be the more general, but often there seems to be little difference between the two forms. There is no genitive singular.

s back to the last-stated noun and is especially common ken German.

elcher can also be an interrogative pronoun (see pp.), an interrogative adjective (see pp. 116–17), and a ve pronoun or adjective (see pp. 139–40).

ee also **irgendwelcher**, p. 151.

enig, *little*; **wenige**, *few*

the basic form and use of **wenig**, see **viel**, pp. 156–7: rything stated there about **viel** (except the sections on **eviel** and the comparative and superlative) also applies to **enig**.

ein wenig, *a little*, is invariable:

> **wir haben nur ein wenig Zeit**, *we only have a little time*

A very little is **ein klein wenig** (the **klein** is also invariable):

> **ein (ganz) klein wenig Zucker, bitte**, *(just) a very little sugar, please*

□ **Viel** is also used, much more commonly, standing without an article in front of a noun. It takes no endings in the singular and the ending in the plural:

> **ich habe so viel Zeit,** *I've so much time*
> **nicht viele Engländer kommen zu un**
> *English visit us*

Viel can also be used as an adjective after an article case it takes normal adjective endings:

> **die vielen guten Weine, die man hier ka**
> **kann,** *the many good wines one can buy h*

□ An adjective following **viel** in the singular behaves as adjective without an article (see pp. 106–7):

> **mit sehr viel schlechtem Wein,** *with a very gi*
> *deal of bad wine*

After **viele** in the plural it behaves like an adjective after another adjective (see p. 108–9):

> **viele ältere Engländer,** *many elderly English*

□ **Wieviel,** *how much* (singular) is written as one word; **wie viele,** *how many* (plural) as two; **soviel** is written as one word when it is a conjunction (= *as far as*), but as two when it means *so much*:

> **soviel ich weiß, hat er nicht so viel Theater**
> **gesehen,** *as far as I know he hasn't seen very much*
> *theatre*

▶ **Viel** has an irregular comparative and superlative (**mehr, meist**). See p. 113.

■ **welcher,** *some; any*

Welcher is declined like **dieser** (see p. 86):

> **wir haben keinen Kaffee mehr, hast du**
> **welchen?,** *we've no coffee left, have you any?*

| Prepositions

Prepositions—words like *in*, *on*, *over*—stand in front of a noun or pronoun to relate it to the rest of the sentence:

> **immer singt er in seinem Bad**, *he always sings in his bath* (preposition: **in**, *in*)

Prepositions can also stand in front of a verb—*without singing*. In English this part of the verb is usually the *-ing* form. In German most prepositions cannot be followed by a verb, and the sentence has to be reconstructed (see Translation Problems, *-ing*, pp. 139–40). Those that can be followed by a verb use the infinitive with **zu**:

> **ohne zu singen**, *without singing*
> **um zu singen**, *in order to sing*

CASE WITH PREPOSITIONS

Prepositions in German are followed by nouns or pronouns in the accusative, the genitive, or the dative.

■ The dative is the case found most frequently after a preposition. In general, if you are not sure what case a preposition takes and are not in a position to look it up, use the dative. The following nine very common prepositions always take the dative, and there are many others:

aus, *out of*	**mit**, *with*
außer, *except; outside*	**nach**, *after; to*
bei, *near; with; at the house of*	**seit**, *since*
gegenüber, *opposite* (follows noun)	**von**, *from; of*
	zu, *to*

■ Seven prepositions always take the accusative:

bis, *until*	**für**, *for*
durch, *through*	**gegen**, *against; towards*
entlang, *along* (following its noun; otherwise dative)	**ohne**, *without*
	um, *round*

There are also a very small number of less common prepositions that always take the accusative.

■ Four common prepositions take the genitive:

(an)statt, *instead of*	**während**, *during*
trotz, *in spite of*	**wegen**, *because of*

Prepositions ending **-seits** (e.g. **diesseits**, *this side of*) and **-halb** (e.g. **innerhalb**, *inside*) can take the genitive, but are more often found followed by **von** + the dative.

A large number of uncommon prepositions and prepositional phrases, including many legal ones, also take the genitive.

■ A group of prepositions take the accusative if motion towards is implied and the dative if not. The prepositions in this group are:

an, *on; at*	**über**, *over*
auf, *on*	**unter**, *under; among*
in, *in*	**vor**, *in front of*
hinter, *behind*	**zwischen**, *between*
neben, *near; beside*	

The only prepositions outside this group that commonly imply motion towards are **zu** and **nach**, with which the case is always dative. So apart from **zu** and **nach**, if a preposition implies motion towards, as a general rule use the accusative.

■ **An**, **auf**, **über**, and **vor**, and less frequently other prepositions, can be used with a figurative meaning after verbs (e.g. **bestehen auf**, *insist on*). In such cases **vor** always takes the dative, **auf** and **über** usually take the accusative, and **an** varies (see pp. 51–2). For more detail on individual prepositions see the Alphabetical List, pp. 163–87. For preposition and case with individual verbs, Oxford Reference: *German Verbs* should be consulted.

■ Where two prepositions joined by **und** or **oder** stand before the same noun it takes the case of the last one:

> **du kommst mit oder ohne deine Schwester?**, *are you coming with or without your sister?*

CONTRACTED FORMS OF PREPOSITIONS

Many prepositions can combine with a following definite article to produce a contraction:

> **wir gehen zum (= zu *dem*) Laden**, *we're going to the shop*

■ Contractions are not used

where the article is stressed (meaning *that*):

> **wir gehen zu *dem* Laden**, *we're going to that shop*

where the noun has an adjective clause that particularizes it:

> **wir gehen zu dem Laden, wo wir immer einkaufen**, *we're going to the shop where we always shop* (i.e. that particular shop)

■ Apart from the above cases the following contracted forms are almost always preferred to the non-contracted forms:

am (an dem)	**vom (von dem)**
beim (bei dem)	**zum (zu dem)**
im (in dem)	**zur (zu der)**
ins (in das)	

In addition, the following contractions are very frequent indeed in spoken German and are very often found in modern printed German:

ans (an das)	**übern (über den)**
aufs (auf das)	**übers (über das)**
außerm (außer dem)	**ums (um das)**
durchs (durch das)	**unterm (unter dem)**
fürs (für das)	**untern (unter den)**
hinterm (hinter dem)	**unters (unter das)**
hintern (hinter den)	**vorm (vor dem)**
hinters (hinter das)	**vors (vor das)**
überm (über dem)	

Other contracted forms may be heard in spoken German:

> **tu's auf'n Tisch**, *put it on the table*

DA + PREPOSITIONS

Da may be prefixed to most prepositions, giving the meaning 'preposition + *it*':

> **von**, *from*→ **davon**, *from it*: **was hast du davon?**,
> *what do you get from it?*

If the preposition begins with a vowel an extra **r** is inserted: **daraus**.

■ These combined forms are only used to refer to things.

◨ The prepositions **außer, bis, gegenüber, ohne, seit** do not have **da-** forms; nor do prepositions that take the genitive.

In questions prepositions combine with **wo** in the same way to give the meaning 'preposition + *what*':

> **wovon?**, *of what?*
> **worüber?**, *about what?*

> **worüber sprichst du?**, *what are you talking about?*

▶ See Interrogative Pronouns, pp. 143–4.

▶ **Wo** combinations can also be used as relatives. See Relative Pronouns, p. 141.

ALPHABETICAL LIST OF GERMAN PREPOSITIONS AND THEIR USE

The use of prepositions differs considerably from language to language. Below we give an alphabetical list of all common German prepositions, and many less common ones, with their main and subsidiary meanings, their cases, and their use. Where a preposition has a number of meanings, the principal meaning is given first, with other meanings following in alphabetical order.

In addition, on pp. 188–94 there is an alphabetical list of English prepositions with their various German equivalents, for cross-reference to the German list.

ab, *from* (time); *from . . . on* (place)

+ dative

> **ab morgen**, *from tomorrow*
> **ab Mainz fuhr der Zug noch langsamer**, *from Mainz on the train went even more slowly*

an, *at*

+ dative (no motion, or motion within) or accusative (motion towards)

at (dative)

> **es ist jemand an der Tür**, *there's someone at the door*
> **er unterrichtet an der Kantschule**, *he teaches at the Kantschule*
> **am Wochenende**, *at the weekend*

at (accusative)

> **er klopfte an die Tür**, *he knocked at the door*

about (dative)

> **das gefällt mir an ihm,** *that's what I like about him*
>
> **was ist daran komisch?,** *what's funny about it?*
>
> **das Schlimmste an der ganzen Sache ist . . . ,** *the worst thing about the whole business is . . .*

by (dative)

> **du erkennst mich an meinem rosa Anorak,** *you'll recognize me by my pink anorak*

of; in respect of (dative)

> **ein Mangel an Geld,** *a lack of money*
>
> **ein großer Aufwand an Zeit,** *a great expenditure of time*
>
> **sie ist reich an Ideen,** *she is rich in (= in respect of) ideas*

on (= *up against*; dative)

> **Frankfurt am Main, . . .** *on the River Main*
>
> **am Ufer des Sees,** *on the bank of the lake*
>
> **der Spiegel hängt an der langen Wand,** *the mirror hangs on the long wall*
>
> **sie gingen am Strand entlang,** *they walked along on the beach*

on (but not literally *on top of*, and no motion towards; dative)

> **er arbeitet an einem neuen Buch,** *he's working on a new book*
>
> **am Sonntag,** *on Sunday*
>
> **am zweiten Februar,** *on the second of February*

on(to) (often, a vertical surface; accusative)

> **schreib es an die Tafel,** *write it on the board*
>
> **er lehnte es an die Wand,** *he leant it on (against) the wall*

to (accusative)

> **an die Arbeit!**, *to work!*
>
> **sie schickte ein Weihnachtsgeschenk an ihre Mutter**, *she sent a Christmas present to her mother*

(an)statt, *instead of*

+ genitive

> **er kam anstatt seines Sohnes**, *he came instead of his son*

Sometimes takes dative instead of genitive, and must do when the noun has no article or adjective in front of it:

> **anstatt Protesten**, *instead of protests*

auf, *on(to)*

+ dative (no motion, or motion within) or accusative (motion towards)

on (dative)

> **es ist so viel Verkehr auf der Straße**, *there's so much traffic on the road*
>
> **sie stand eine Zeitlang auf dem Marktplatz**, *she stood for a time on (in) the market square*

on(to) (accusative)

> **er ging auf die Straße hinaus**, *he went out onto the street*
>
> **sie legte sich auf das Bett**, *she lay down on the bed*

at (accusative)

> **sie machte es auf meinen Wunsch (meine Bitte)**, *she did it at my wish (my request)*

for (+ future time; accusative)

> **sie kommt auf eine Woche**, *she's coming for a week*

in

> **der Vogel saß auf einem Baum**, *the bird was sitting in a tree*
>
> **auf keine Weise**, *in no way*
>
> **auf englisch**, *in English*
>
> **auf jeden Fall**, *come what may* (= *in any possible case*)

of (accusative)

> **ich habe keine Hoffnung (keine Aussicht) auf eine Antwort**, *I've no hope (no prospect) of an answer*
>
> **sie war immer eifersüchtig (neidisch; stolz) auf mich**, *she was always jealous (envious; proud) of me*

to (accusative)

> **die Antwort auf meine Frage**, *the answer to my question*
>
> **du hast kein Recht auf einen Paß**, *you have no right to a passport*

aus, *out of*

+ dative

out of

> **er stieg aus dem Auto**, *he got out of the car*
>
> **trink nicht aus der Flasche!**, *don't drink out of the bottle*
>
> **sie tat es aus Stolz**, *she did it out of pride*

from

> **aus welcher Richtung kommt der Wind?**, *which direction is the wind coming from?*

woher kommst du?—Aus Bremen, *where are you from?—From Bremen*

made of

ein Kaffeetisch aus Holz, *a coffee-table made of wood*

außer, *except*

+ dative

except; apart from

ich habe kein Karo außer dem As, *I haven't a diamond except (apart from) the ace*

außer uns war niemand da, *nobody was there except us*

beyond

seine Treue ist außer Zweifel, *his loyalty is beyond doubt*

out of

diese Bahn ist außer Betrieb, *this tram is out of service*

seine Kinder waren außer Kontrolle, *his children were out of control*

ich bin außer Atem, *I'm out of breath*

außerhalb, *outside*

+ genitive

er wohnt außerhalb der Stadt, *he lives outside the town*

Often takes **von** + dative instead of genitive:

er wohnt außerhalb von der Stadt

bei, *at the house of*

+ dative

at the house of

> **Sahne kannst du beim Bäcker kaufen,** *you can buy cream at the baker's*
>
> **bei uns (zu Hause),** *at our house; at home*
>
> **wir sind bei Kaisers eingeladen,** *we're invited to the Kaisers'*

To the house of is **zu** (**bei** can't be used with a verb of motion):

> **wir gehen zu Kaisers,** *we're going to the Kaisers'*

at

> **beim Frühstück,** *at breakfast*
>
> **bei der Arbeit,** *at work*
>
> **bei der bloßen Idee,** *at the very idea*
>
> **bei nächster Gelegenheit,** *at the next opportunity*

by; near

> **bleib bei mir!,** *stay by me*
>
> **sie saß beim Feuer,** *she sat by the fire*
>
> **Gräfelfing bei München,** *Gräfelfing near Munich*

for (= in spite of)

> **bei allen seiner Tugenden ist er kein liebenswerter Mensch,** *for all his virtues he's not a lovable person*
>
> **bei alledem,** *for all that*

in

> **bei gutem Wetter,** *in fine weather*
>
> **bei schlechter Laune,** *in a bad mood*

with

> **bei Norddeutschen ist der Fall anders,** *with north Germans the case is different*

bei diesen Preisen kann man sich kaum was leisten, *with prices like these you can hardly afford anything*

beiderseits, *on both sides of*

+ genitive

beiderseits der Straße, *on both sides of the street*

Often takes **von** + dative instead of genitive:

beiderseits von der Straße

betreffend, *with regard to*

+ accusative; commercial German; less common; usually follows noun or pronoun

Ihr Fax betreffend . . ., *with regard to your fax . . .*

bis, *until; as far as*

+ accusative

until

bis jetzt habe ich nichts gesehen, *I've seen nothing until now*
warte nur bis nächsten Frühling, *just wait until next spring*
bis Sonnabend!, *see you on (= goodbye until) Saturday*

When a noun with an article follows **bis**, **bis zu** + dative is used:

bis zum dritten Oktober, *until the third of October*
geh bis zur Kreuzung, *go on until (go as far as) the crossroads*

The negative of **bis**, *not until*, is **erst** + **um**, **erst an**, etc.:

> **erst um drei Uhr**, *not until three o'clock*
> **erst am dritten Mai**, *not until the third of May*

by

> **bis übermorgen ist es fertig**, *it'll be ready by the day after tomorrow*

bis auf, *except (for)*

+ accusative

> **wir sind alle durchgefallen bis auf die drei Mädchen**, *we all failed except (for) the three girls*

dank, *thanks to*

+ dative (occasionally genitive); less common

> **dank Ihrer Hilfe bin ich heute noch am Leben**, *thanks to your help I am still alive today*

diesseits, *on this side of*

+ genitive

> **diesseits des Flusses**, *on this side of the river*

Often takes **von** + dative instead of genitive:

> **diesseits vom Fluß**

durch, *through; by*

+ accusative

through

> **sie watete durch den Bach**, *she waded through the stream*
> **sie marschierten durch die Stadt**, *they marched through the town*
> **es kam durch das Fenster**, *it came through the window*

by

> **du hast es durch deine Briefe klargemacht,**
> *you've made it clear by your letters*
>
> **er ist durch Schnee aufgehalten worden,** *he was*
> *held up by snow*

By is **durch** in passive constructions where a thing is referred to as
the cause; where it is a person, **von** is used. See Passive, pp. 30–1.

eingerechnet, *including*

+ accusative; less common; usually follows noun or pronoun

> **die zwei Flaschen Wein (mit) eingerechnet,**
> *including the two bottles of wine*

entlang, *along*

+ accusative; usually follows noun or pronoun—takes dative if
it precedes

> **sie schlenderte die Straße entlang,** *she strolled*
> *along the road*
> **entlang dem Kanal,** *along the canal*

entsprechend, *corresponding to*

+ dative; commercial German; less common; usually follows a
noun or pronoun

> **unseren Erwartungen entsprechend,**
> *corresponding to our expectations*

für, *for*

+ accusative

> **ich habe die Blumen für dich gebracht,** *I've*
> *brought the flowers for you*

ich habe sie am Bahnhof für zehn Mark gekauft,
I bought them for ten marks at the station

das ist sehr leicht für mich, *that's very easy for me*

Was für ein means *what sort of*. The **für** does not affect the
case of **ein**: the **ein** declines according to its job in the
sentence:

mit was für einem Kuli schreibst du?, *what sort of*
a ballpoint are you writing with?

gegen, *against*

+ accusative

against

er war immer gegen die EG, *he was always against*
the EC

er lehnte die Leiter gegen die Mauer, *he leant the*
ladder against the wall

hätten Sie etwas dagegen, wenn wir etwas
später essen würden?, *would you have anything*
against our eating a little later?

es geschah gegen alle unsere Hoffnungen, *it*
happened against all our hopes

about (with numbers)

gegen dreihundert Soldaten, *about 300 soldiers*

compared to

gegen dich bin ich nichts, *I'm nothing compared to you*

for (= *in exchange for*)

das bekommen Sie nur gegen Bargeld, *you only*
get that for ready cash

towards (usually with time)

gegen fünf Uhr, *towards five o'clock*

gegenüber, *opposite*

+ dative; follows a pronoun, usually follows a noun

opposite

> **die Sparkasse liegt dem Kino gegenüber
> (gegenüber dem Kino)**, *the savings bank is
> opposite the cinema*

compared to

> **dir gegenüber bin ich ein Anfänger**, *I'm a beginner
> compared to you*

towards

> **unsere Haltung gegenüber den neuen
> Bundesländern**, *our attitude towards the new
> federal states*

gemäß; zufolge, *in accordance with*

both: + dative; formal; less common; usually follow noun or
pronoun

> **Ihren Befehlen gemäß / zufolge**, *in accordance
> with your commands*

hinter, *behind*; *beyond*

+ dative (no motion, or motion within) or accusative (motion
towards)

behind (dative)

> **der Garten liegt hinter dem Haus**, *the garden is
> behind the house*
> **du darfst hier hinter dem Haus spielen**, *you can
> play here behind the house*
> **aber nicht hinter dem Zaun!**, *but not beyond the
> fence!*

behind (accusative)

> **geh schnell hinter die Mauer!**, *get behind the wall quickly*

in, *in*; *into*

+ dative (no motion, or motion within) or accusative (motion towards)

in (dative)

> **wir essen immer im Wohnzimmer**, *we always eat in the living-room*
>
> **er lief im Wohnzimmer umher**, *he ran about in the living-room*
>
> **im Winter**, *in winter*
>
> **im Januar**, *in January*
>
> **in fünf Minuten**, *in five minutes*

into (accusative)

> **er lief schnell ins Wohnzimmer**, *he ran quickly into the living-room*
>
> **sie tanzten bis tief in die Nacht hinein**, *they danced deep into the night*

to (accusative)

> **gehen wir in die Kirche oder ins Kino?**, *shall we go to church or to the cinema?*
>
> **in die Vereinigten Staaten**, *to the USA* (only non-neuter names of countries; see pp. 176–7)

innerhalb, *inside*; *within*

+ genitive

> **innerhalb des Schlosses**, *inside the castle*

Often takes **von** + dative instead of genitive:

innerhalb vom Schloß

. . . and must take **von** when the noun has no article or
adjective before it:

innerhalb von drei Stunden, *within three hours*

jenseits, *on the other side of; beyond*

+ genitive

jenseits des Todes, *beyond death*

Often takes **von** + dative instead of genitive:

jenseits vom Tod

laut, *according to*

+ dative or genitive; less common; newspaper and TV language

laut unseren (unsrer) letzten Meldungen,
according to our latest reports

mit, *with*

+ dative

with

Obsttorte mit Schlagsahne, *fruit flan with whipped
cream*
ich bin mit meinem Mann gekommen, *I'm here
with my husband*
kommst du mit?, *are you coming with us/me?*
iß das mit deiner Gabel!, *eat it with your fork*

at

mit 60 km/h (= Stundenkilometern) fahren, *to
travel at 60 k.p.h.*
mit 18 (Jahren), *at eighteen*

by

> **fährst du mit dem Bus?**, *are you going by bus?*
> **es kam mit der Post**, *it came by post*

nach, *after*

+ dative

after

> **nach deinem Examen**, *after your exam*
> **nach der Schule**, *after school*
> **er kam uns nach**, *he came after us* (**nachkommen**)
> **ein Tag nach dem anderen**, *one day after another*
> **zwanzig nach vier**, *twenty past* (= *after*) *four*

according to

> **nach Shakespeare**, *according to Shakespeare*
> **nach Geschmack**, *according to taste*
> **nach meiner Uhr ist es schon drei**, *by* (= *according to*) *my watch it's already three*
> **meiner Meinung nach**, *in* (= *according to*) *my opinion* (note position of **nach** in this set phrase)

for

> **die Sehnsucht (der Wunsch; der Verlangen; die Suche) nach politischer Macht**, *the longing (the wish; the craving; the search) for political power*

to (with countries, towns, continents)

> **wir fahren nach England**, *we're travelling to England*
> **eine Reise nach Berlin**, *a journey to Berlin*
> **nächstes Jahr geht's nach Australien**, *next year we're off to Australia*

But before countries used with the definite article (i.e. feminine ones, plus the very few plural or masculine ones) **in** is used:

in die Türkei, *to Turkey*
in die USA, *to the USA* (**nach** is also found)
in den Jemen, *to the Yemen*

Spoken north German extends this use of **nach** = *to* to many
other places:

er ist nach der Bushaltestelle gelaufen, *he walked
to the bus stop*

to the (with compass points, directions)

nach Süden (also **in den**), *to the south*
nach rechts, *to the right*
nach oben, *to the top; upstairs*

towards

sie sah nach der offenen Tür, *she looked towards
the open door*
er ging langsam nach dem Fluß zu, *he went slowly
towards the river*
nach Hause, *(to) home*

neben, *beside; next to*

+ dative (no motion, or motion within) or accusative (motion
towards)

beside (dative)

er saß dicht neben mir, *he was sitting right beside
(next to) me*
sie ging neben mir auf der Straße, *she was walking
beside me on the street* (no motion relative to me)

beside (accusative)

er setzte sich dicht neben mich, *he sat down right
beside me*
stell die Flasche neben die anderen, *put the bottle
beside (next to) the others*

besides (dative)

> **neben den Butterbroten brauchen wir auch Wein,**
> *besides (as well as) the sandwiches we need wine too*

oberhalb, *above*

+ genitive; less common

> **oberhalb der Berghütte,** *above the mountain hut*

Often takes **von** + dative instead of genitive:

> **oberhalb von der Berghütte**

ohne, *without*

+ accusative

> **ohne Hoffnung,** *without hope*
> **ohne Hut,** *without a hat*
> **ohne seinen Hut,** *without his hat*

The indefinite article (but not possessives, etc.) is omitted after **ohne**.

per, *per, by*; pro, *per*

+ accusative; less common

> **per Luftpost,** *by airmail*
> **dreimal pro Woche,** *three times a (per) week*

Neither of these prepositions takes an article, so the accusative that follows them is usually hidden.

seit, *since*

+ dative

since

> **er ist hier seit Montag,** *he's been here since Monday*

ich habe sie seit Ostern nicht mehr gesehen,
I haven't seen her again since Easter

for

seit zwei Monaten, *for three months*
seit einiger Zeit, *for some time*

■ Note the tenses used with **seit**:

du ißt seit einer Stunde, *you've been eating for an hour*

du ißt seit halb eins, *you've been eating since 12.30*

For an action or state starting in the past and going on to the present, **seit** + present tense is used (the English is the perfect continuous). **Seit** can have either of its two meanings.

With a negative, or a series of actions, the perfect is used, as in English:

du hast seit einer Stunde nichts gegessen, *you haven't eaten anything for an hour*

seit halb eins hast du drei Brötchen und vier Bockwürste gegessen, *since half past twelve you've eaten three rolls and four sausages*

□ The above also applies to an action starting before some point in the past and continuing to that point. This produces **seit** + the past tense:

er war seit einer Stunde dort, *he had been there for an hour*

The English tense here is the pluperfect. With a negative or a series of actions the German also uses the pluperfect:

er war seit Weihnachten dreimal in Frankfurt gewesen, *he had been to Frankfurt three times since Christmas*

statt, *instead of*

+ genitive (shortened form of **anstatt**; identical in use)

▶ See **anstatt**, p. 165.

trotz, *in spite of*

+ genitive

> **er kam trotz des Regens**, *he came in spite of the rain*

Often takes dative instead of genitive, and must do when the noun has no article or adjective in front of it:

> **trotz Karten und Briefen**, *in spite of cards and letters*

And note the datives in **trotz allem**, *in spite of everything*, and **trotzdem**, *in spite of that*.

über, *over; above*

+ dative (no motion, or motion within) or accusative (motion towards)

over; above (dative)

> **das Bild hängt über dem Fernseher**, *the picture hangs over the television*
> **Wasservögel kreisten über dem See**, *waterfowl were circling above (over) the lake*

over (accusative)

> **wir fahren hier über die Bahn**, *here we go over the railway*
> **über eine halbe Stunde**, *over half an hour*
> **über Weihnachten**, *over Christmas*
> **ein Wettlauf über 1000 Meter**, *a race over 1000 metres*

about (accusative)

> **ich muß darüber nachdenken,** *I must think about that*
>
> **wissen Sie etwas über Raupen?,** *do you know anything about caterpillars?*
>
> **er hielt einen Vortrag über Raupen,** *he gave a lecture about caterpillars*

via (accusative)

> **fahren Sie über Hamburg?,** *are you going via Hamburg?*
>
> **er ist über die Autobahn gekommen,** *he came via (along) the motorway*

um, *round; around*

+ accusative

(a)round

> **sie kam um die Ecke,** *she came round the corner*
>
> **um 1900,** *around 1900*

Um is often strengthened by adding **rings** or **rund** before it or **herum** after it (or both):

> **rund um die Stadt herum lief eine Mauer,** *right round the town ran a wall*

at (with clock times)

> **um sieben Uhr,** *at seven o'clock*
>
> **um Mittag,** *at noon*

▶ See Time, p. 208.

by

> **ich muß den Termin um eine Woche verschieben,** *I have to postpone the appointment by a week*
>
> **es ist um drei Meter länger als das andere,** *it's longer by three metres than the other one*

for

> **der Kampf um das tägliche Brot**, *the fight for one's daily bread*
>
> **wir spielen nicht um Geld**, *we're not playing for money*
>
> **eine Bitte um Hilfe**, *a request for help*
>
> **ich habe Angst um mein Leben**, *I fear for my life*

for the sake of (**um** + genitive + **willen**)

> **um Himmels willen tu das nicht!**, *don't do it, for heaven's sake!*

unter, *below; under*

+ dative (no motion, or motion within) or accusative (motion towards)

below; under (dative)

> **wir wohnen unter Schmidts**, *we live below the Schmidts*
>
> **sie tanzten unter freiem Himmel**, *they danced under the open sky*

below; under (accusative)

> **wir setzten uns unter eine Eiche**, *we sat down under an oak*

among (dative)

> **wir sind unter Freunden**, *we're among friends*

among (accusative)

> **du gehst nicht oft genug unter Leute in deinem Alter**, *you don't mix with (go among) people of your own age enough*

given (dative)

> **unter diesen Umständen**, *in (= given) these circumstances*
>
> **unter einer Bedingung**, *on (= given) one condition*

under (= *at less than*; dative)

> **unter hundert Mark verkauf' ich's nicht!**, *I'm not selling it under 100 DM*

unterhalb, *below*

+ genitive; less common

> **er wohnt irgendwo unterhalb der Kantstraße**, *he lives somewhere below Kantstraße*

Sometimes takes **von** + dative instead of genitive:

> **unterhalb von der Kantstraße**

von, *from*

+ dative

from

> **ich habe das Geld von meinem Vater erhalten**, *I received the money from my father*
>
> **gehst du jetzt von hier weg?**, *are you going away from here now?*
>
> **von Morgen bis in die Nacht**, *from morning till night*
>
> **von hier aus kannst du drei Grafschaften sehen**, *from (up) here you can see three counties*
>
> **von mir aus kannst du es sofort tun**, *from my point of view (as far as I'm concerned) you can do it straight away*

about

> **was hältst du davon?**, *what do you think about it?*
>
> **ich schwärme (bin begeistert) von deinem neuen Auto**, *I'm mad about your new car*

by (in passive constructions)

> **es ist schon von der Putzfrau gemacht worden**, *it has already been done by the cleaning lady* (see Passive, pp. 30–1)

of

>> **der Geruch von Zwiebeln**, *the smell of onions*
>> **der Prinz von Dänemark**, *the Prince of Denmark*
>> **ein Kind von vier Jahren**, *a child of four*
>> **das ist furchtbar nett von Ihnen**, *that's awfully kind of you*

Von (= *of*) is also very frequently used instead of the genitive in spoken German; the genitive is seen as literary or affected:

>> **die Tante meines Freundes → die Tante von meinem Freund**, *my friend's aunt*

vor, *in front of*

+ dative (no motion, or motion within) or accusative (motion towards)

in front of (dative)

>> **draußen vorm Haus stand eine Straßenlaterne**, *outside in front of the house stood a streetlamp*
>> **er ging zwei Schritte vor mir**, *he walked two paces in front of me* (no motion relative to me)

in front of (accusative)

>> **stell dein Auto vor die Polizeiwache**, *leave your car in front of the police station*

before (dative)

>> **vor Sonnenuntergang**, *before sunset*
>> **vor dem letzten Krieg**, *before the last war*
>> **zehn Minuten vor zehn**, *ten to* (= *before*) *ten*

of (= *in the face of; as a consequence of*)

>> **sie stirbt vor Hunger**, *she's dying of hunger*
>> **ich habe Angst vor Stieren**, *I'm afraid of bulls*
>> **vor Stieren muß man immer auf der Hut sein**, *you must always beware of bulls*

> **da war keine Warnung vor Stieren**, *there was no warning of bulls*

with; for (with emotions; dative)

> **er strahlte vor Freude**, *he beamed with joy*
> **ich konnte vor Aufregung nicht denken**, *I couldn't think for excitement*

während, *during*

+ genitive

during

> **es geschah während des Kriegs**, *it happened during the war*

Sometimes takes dative instead of genitive, and must do when the noun has no article or adjective in front of it:

> **während drei Jahren**, *for three years*

wegen, *because of*

+ genitive; in literary German may follow its noun

because of

> **wir sind nur wegen des guten Wetters hier**, *we're only here because of the fine weather*

on . . . 's account

> **tu das nicht wegen meines Mannes!**, *don't do it on my husband's account*

Sometimes takes dative instead of genitive, and must do with a pronoun or when the noun has no article or adjective in front of it:

> **tu das nicht wegen mir!**, *don't do it on my account!*
> **bloß wegen ein paar Leuten**, *just because of a few people*

The compound forms **meinetwegen**, **deinetwegen**, etc. are also used instead of **wegen mir**, **wegen dir**, etc.

Von wegen + dative is used in colloquial German to mean *about*:

> **erzähl mir nichts von wegen Lohnsteuer!**, *don't talk to me about income tax!*

wider, *against*

+ accusative; less common; literary

> **ich tat es wider Willen**, *I did it against my will*

zu, *to*

+ dative

to

> **ich fahre zu meiner Tante in Ostfriesland**, *I'm going to my aunt in Ostfriesland*
> **ich fahre zum Flughafen**, *I'm driving to the airport*
> **du gehst zu Bett!**, *you're going to bed now*
> **er geht zur Schule**, *he goes to school*
> **du bist zum Abendessen eingeladen**, *you're invited to supper*
> **kommen Sie zur Sache!**, *come to the point!*

at

> **zu Ostern und zu Weihnachten**, *at Easter and Christmas*
> **zu Hause**, *at home*
> **die da zu drei Mark, bitte**, *those at three marks, please*
> **der Römer zu Frankfurt**, *the Römer (town-hall) at Frankfurt*

for

> **meine Neigung (Freundschaft; Liebe) zu Ihnen**, *my liking (friendship; love) for you*

bist du zum Essen fertig?, *are you ready to eat (= for eating)?*

zum zweiten Mal, *for the second time*

was kriegst du zu Weihnachten (deinem Geburtstag)?, *what are you getting for Christmas (your birthday)?*

zufolge, *in accordance with*

▶ See **gemäß**, p. 173.

zuliebe, *for the sake of*

+ dative; less common; follows noun or pronoun

tu es mir zuliebe, *do it for my sake*

zwischen, *between*

+ dative (no motion, or motion within) or accusative (motion towards)

between (dative)

sie stand zwischen mir und ihrem Bruder, *she was standing between her brother and me*

sie ging zwischen mir und ihrem Bruder, *she was walking between her brother and me* (no motion relative to us)

between (accusative)

das Auto fuhr zwischen die Eingangssäulen und in die große Garage, *the car drove between the entrance pillars and into the big garage*

CROSS-REFERENCE LIST OF ENGLISH PREPOSITIONS

Prepositions presenting problems of translation are listed. These prepositions are cross-referenced to the list of German prepositions starting on p. 163. It is dangerous to take a German meaning from the list that follows without subsequently checking its usage in the German list.

about
  an, 164
  über, 181
  von, 183
  with numbers, **gegen**, 172

above
  oberhalb, 178
  über, 180

according to
  laut, 175
  nach, 176

after
  nach, 176

against
  gegen, 172
  wider, 186

along
  entlang, 171

among
  unter, 182

apart from
  außer, 167

around
  um, 181

as . . . as in comparisons
  so . . . wie. See p. 114.

as far as
  bis, 169

as well as
  neben, 178

at
  an, 163
  auf, 165
  bei, 168
  mit, 175
  zu, 186
  with clock times, **um**, 181

at the house of
  bei, 168

because of
  wegen, 185

before
  vor, 184

behind
  hinter, 173–4

below
  unter, 182
  unterhalb, 183

beside
  neben, 177

besides
  neben, 178

between
  zwischen, 187

instead of
  (an)statt, 165

into
  in, 174

made of
  aus, 167

near
  bei, 168

next to
  neben, 177

not until
  see **bis**, 169–70

of
  von, 184
  = *in the face of*, **vor**, 184–5

on
  auf, 165
  = *up against*, **an**, 164
  = *given*, **unter**, 182
  non-literal, **an**, 164

on . . . 's account
  wegen, 185

on both sides of
  beiderseits, 169

on the other side of
  jenseits, 175

on this side of
  diesseits, 170

on(to)
  an, 164
  auf, 165

towards
  gegenüber, 173
  nach, 177
  with time, **gegen**, 172

under
  unter, 182

until
  bis, 166

via
  über, 181

with
  bei, 168–9
  mit, 175
  + emotion, **vor**, 185

within
  innerhalb, 174

without
  ohne, 178

with regard to
  betreffend, 169

| Conjunctions

Conjunctions are joining-words. They may join nouns or pronouns:

> **sie oder ihr Hund**, *she or her dog* (conjunction: **oder**)

or phrases:

> **ein sehr aufgeregter und doch noch arbeitender**
> **Beamter**, *an official, very excited and yet still*
> *working* (conjunction: **und**)

or two or more main clauses:

> **er singt, aber er kann nicht spielen**, *he sings, but*
> *he can't play* (conjunction: **aber**)

A conjunction like this that can join two main clauses together is called a coordinating conjunction.

Some conjunctions introduce subordinate clauses:

> **ich tue es, sobald ich das Geld habe**, *I'll do it as*
> *soon as I have the money* (conjunction: **sobald**)

This sort of conjunction is called a subordinating conjunction.

COORDINATING CONJUNCTIONS

In German there are six common coordinating conjunctions. When these conjunctions introduce a clause they are followed by normal word order—i.e. subject, verb, rest of sentence. See Word Order, p. 215.

They are:

aber, *but*	**oder**, *or*
allein, *only; but*	**sondern**, *but (on the contrary)*
denn, *for*	**und**, *and*

Nearly all other conjunctions are subordinating conjunctions (see p. 197).

■ **Aber** can also be an adverb, meaning *however*:

> **ihr Zug war verspätet, sie ist aber angekommen,** *her train was late; she's arrived, however, (or, but she's arrived)*

■ **Allein** explains why something didn't happen:

> **ich hatte mitfahren wollen, allein ich war erkältet,** *I had wanted to go with them, only (but) I had a cold*

It is rather literary: **aber** is usually used in this sense in spoken German.

■ **Oder** is also used in *either . . . or* sentences: **entweder . . . oder**:

> **entweder bezahlt er die Rechnung, oder er bekommt die Sachen nicht,** *either he pays the bill or he doesn't get the goods*
> **entweder Sie bezahlen, oder ich rufe die Polizei,** *either you pay or I call the police*

Note the two possible word orders in the **entweder** half of the sentence. There is a difference in tone: inversion after **entweder**, no threat; normal order after **entweder**, threat!

The opposite of **entweder . . . oder** is **weder . . . noch**, *neither . . . nor*. Both **weder** and **noch** are adverbs, and both must be followed by inversion:

> **weder bezahle ich, noch werden Sie die Polizei rufen,** *I shall neither pay, nor will you call the police*

■ **Sondern** always follows a negative and has the sense of a correction: '*not this but, on the contrary, that*'. Compare:

> **das ist nicht wahr, sondern (es ist) falsch,** *that's not true, but false*
> **das ist nicht wahr, aber es ist interessant,** *that's not true, but it's interesting*

Not only . . . but also is **nicht nur . . . sondern auch**:

> **nicht nur ist es furchtbar einfach, sondern man kann es jetzt auch sehr preiswert bekommen,** *not only is it very easy, but you can now also get it very cheaply*

Nicht nur is an adverb, followed by inversion; **sondern** is a coordinating conjunction followed by normal order; and the **auch** stands as an adverb later in the second clause.

SUBORDINATING CONJUNCTIONS

Apart from the conjunctions listed above all others are subordinating: they send the verb to the end of the clause. See Word Order, p. 222.

If the clause introduced by a subordinating conjunction stands first in the sentence, the main-clause verb stands immediately after it. See Word Order, p. 216.

Question words (**wo**, **wann**, etc.) can also be used as subordinating conjunctions in order to introduce indirect questions:

> **wann kommt er?,** *when is he coming?*
> **ich frage mich, wann er kommt,** *I wonder when he's coming*

Problems of some subordinating conjunctions

■ **Als, wenn, wann,** *when*

□ **Als** is only used to mean '*when, on one occasion in the past*':

> **als er anrief, wußte ich sofort, wer es war,** *when he phoned I knew straight away who it was*

□ **Wenn** means *when* in the present and future:

> **wenn er anruft, werde ich ihm die Wahrheit sagen,** *when he phones I'll tell him the truth*

However, **wenn** can also mean *if*; if there is ambiguity, use **sobald**, *as soon as*, for *when*:

> **sobald er anruft, werde ich ihm die Wahrheit sagen**

☐ **Wenn** is also used to mean *'when, on more than one occasion in the past'*. If there is ambiguity in this sense of **wenn**, use **sooft**, *as often as*:

> **er rief an, wenn er konnte / sooft er konnte**, *he phoned when(ever) he could*

☐ **Wann** is the question word *when*, also used in indirect questions:

> **wann ruft er an?**, *when is he phoning?*
> **ich weiß nicht, wann er anruft**, *I don't know when he's phoning*

☐ After time expressions (*the day when . . . , the moment when . . .*), **als** and **wenn** may be used for *when*, but **wo** is also frequently found:

> **der Tag, als er ankam / wo er ankam**, *the day when he arrived*

■ **Bis**, *until*; **erst als, erst wenn**, *not until*

Bis is both a preposition and a subordinating conjunction:

> **bis morgen**, *until tomorrow* (preposition)
> **bis wir kommen**, *until we come* (conjunction)

▶ See pp. 169–70 for **bis** as a preposition.

☐ The negative of **bis** the conjunction (*not until*) is **erst als** or **erst wenn** (see p. 197 for the difference between **als** and **wenn**):

> **erst wenn wir kommen, wird er fahren dürfen**, *not until we come will he be allowed to leave*
> **erst als wir kamen, durfte er fahren**, *not until we came was he allowed to leave*

Notice what happens when the 'not until' clause stands second in the sentence:

> **er wird erst fahren dürfen, wenn wir kommen,**
> *he will not be allowed to leave until we come*

□ **Bis** can also mean *by the time that*:

> **bis du kommst, habe ich alles aufgegessen,** *by the time you come I'll have eaten everything*

■ **Seit(dem),** *since*

Seitdem is the conjunction corresponding to the preposition **seit,** *since*. Seit can also be used as a conjunction, but **seitdem** is more common.

The tenses used with **seit(dem)** are the same in all respects as those used with **seit** the preposition (see Prepositions, pp. 178–9):

□ Events start in the past, continue to present . . .

Both clauses are in the present tense in German (both perfect in English):

> **seitdem ich hier wohne, bin ich viel glücklicher,** *since I've been living here I've been much happier*

With a negative main clause, the main clause is in the perfect, the **seitdem** clause in the present tense (both perfect in English):

> **seitdem ich hier wohne, habe ich keinen Menschen gesehen,** *since I've been living here I've seen no one*

□ Events start in the past, continue to the point in the past we are talking about . . .

Both clauses are in the past tense in German (both pluperfect in English):

> **seitdem ich dort wohnte, war ich viel glücklicher,** *since I'd been living there, I'd been much happier*

With a negative main clause, the main clause is in the pluperfect, the **seitdem** clause in the past tense (both pluperfect in English):

> **seitdem ich dort wohnte, hatte ich keinen Menschen gesehen,** *since I'd been living here I'd seen no one*

Numbers, Time, Measurements

CARDINAL NUMBERS

The cardinal numbers are

0	null	19	neunzehn
1	ein (eins when counting)	20	zwanzig
2	zwei (often zwo in speech)	21	einundzwanzig
3	drei	22	zweiundzwanzig ...
4	vier	30	dreißig
5	fünf	40	vierzig
6	sechs	50	fünfzig
7	sieben	60	sechzig
8	acht	70	siebzig
9	neun	80	achtzig
10	zehn	90	neunzig
11	elf	100	(ein)hundert
12	zwölf	101	(ein)hundert(und)eins ...
13	dreizehn	200	zweihundert ...
14	vierzehn	1000	(ein)tausend
15	fünfzehn	1001	tausendeins ...
16	sechzehn	2000	zweitausend ...
17	siebzehn	1 000 000	eine Million ...
18	achtzehn	1 000 000 000	eine Milliarde

■ Number punctuation

□ There are no commas between numbers in German; instead
a space is left. This space is often (but not always) omitted with
units of thousands:

9000 but **10 000**

Very occasionally numbers are found printed with full stops instead of spaces.

☐ Telephone numbers are split up into (and spoken in) pairs:

> **54 78 34, vierundfünfzig achtundsiebzig vierunddreißig**

☐ The centuries (except millennia) are counted in hundreds:

> **im Jahre neunzehnhundertneunundneunzig,** *in 1999*

but: **im Jahre zweitausend,** *in 2000*

☐ Numbers up to but not including **eine Million** are written as a single word:

> **zwei Millionen**
>
> **dreihundertsiebentausendneunhundertneunundneunzig,** *2,307,999*

Such monster written forms are avoided wherever possible; a space or hyphen is sometimes found after **-tausend**.

■ **Ein** has an **-s** when counting, in arithmetic, and when used after a noun (**Zimmer eins,** *room one*); otherwise it declines like the indefinite article. At the end of compounds, however (**hunderteins** etc.), it has the **-s** form even when standing before a noun. Unlike the indefinite article, **ein** = *one* is stressed in spoken German.

One can be a pronoun, in which case it is **einer, eine, ein(e)s**, declined like **dieser** (see Indefinites, p. 148):

> **nimm ein(e)s von den beiden!,** *take one of the two*

■ As well as their numerical-adjective forms above, **das Hundert** and **das Tausend** are also nouns, used in such contexts as **viele Tausende von Menschen,** *many thousands of people*. **Die Million** and **die Milliarde** only have noun forms. They both take a plural **-(e)n**; this plural form is also used when counting.

■ Note the colloquial form **zig-**, *umpteen*: **zighundert,** *umpteen hundred,* **zigtausend,** *umpteen thousand*.

■ Indeclinable forms in **-er** are used in the following cases; the nouns are masculine:

> **ein Fünfziger**, *a 50-mark note*
>
> **ein Dreiundneunziger**, *a '93 wine*
>
> **in den achtziger Jahren**, *in the eighties*

ORDINAL NUMBERS

Ordinal numbers (*first, second, third,* etc.) are formed by adding **-t** to the cardinal number (up to and including **neunzehnt-**, *nineteenth*) or **-st** (from **zwanzigst-**, *twentieth*, on). **Erst-**, *first*, **dritt-**, *third*, **siebt-**, *seventh*, and **acht-**, *eighth*, are irregular.

> **erst-**
>
> **zweit-** (often **zwot-** in conversation, by analogy with **zwo**)
>
> **dritt-**
>
> **viert-** . . .
>
> **sechst-**
>
> **siebt-** (**siebent-** exists but sounds old-fashioned)
>
> **acht-**
>
> **neunt-** . . .
>
> **zwanzigst-**
>
> **einundzwanzigst-** . . .
>
> **dreißigst-** . . .
>
> **(ein)hundertst-**
>
> **(ein)hundert(und)erst-** . . .
>
> **millionst-**

■ Ordinals are adjectives. They always have endings.

■ Ordinals compound with superlatives:

> **das zweitkleinste Bundesland**, *the second smallest Federal State*

They also form adverbs with **-ens**:

> **drittens**, *thirdly*

See p. 206.

■ The German order with **erst-** (and **letzt-**) used with a
cardinal number is often the reverse of the English:

> **die drei ersten (letzten) Wagen**, *the first (last) three
> coaches*

The English order (**die ersten drei**) is also possible.

■ To abbreviate ordinals a full stop or occasionally **(s)t-** is
used, thus:

> **zweite: 2.; II.; 2te**
> **zwanzigste: 20.; XX.; 20ste**

Roman numerals + full stop are used for the names of kings:

> **Heinrich V.**, *Heinrich V*

■ The ordinals are used with **zu** and without any ending to
mean *in . . . s*:

> **zu zweit**, *in twos*; **zu dritt**, *in threes*, etc.

In ones is **einzeln**.

FRACTIONS

Fractions are formed by adding **-el** to the ordinal. They have a
small letter as (indeclinable) adjectives, a capital as (neuter)
nouns. Whole number + fraction is frequently written as a
single word:

> **ein achtel Liter**, *an eighth of a litre*
> **ein Viertel Leberwurst**, *a quarter of liver sausage*
> **Viertel vor eins**, *a quarter to one*
> **eineinviertel**, *one and a quarter*
>
> **das Ganze**, *the whole*
> **ein halb / die Hälfte**, ½
> **ein drittel**, ⅓
> **ein viertel**, ¼
> **ein hundertstel**, ¹⁄₁₀₀

> **drei siebtel**, ⅜
> **anderthalb / ein(und)einhalb**, 1½
> **zweieinhalb**, 2½

Compounds of **-halb** (**anderthalb**, etc.) take no endings.

■ **Halb** and **Hälfte**

ein halb- = *half a*

> **ein halbes Dutzend Eier**, *half a dozen eggs*

die Hälfte = *half (of)*

> **die Hälfte meines Vermögens**, *half my money*

halb = *half (adverb)*

> **meine Arbeit is nur halb fertig**, *my work is only half finished*

■ Decimals are written (and spoken) with a comma rather than a decimal point:

> **11,704: elf Komma sieben null vier**, or **elfkommasiebennullvier**, *11·704*

■ The basic mathematical signs are:

+	**und; plus**	+	**(geteilt) durch**
−	**weniger; minus**	^{2}	**hoch zwei**
×	**mal**	%	**Prozent**

> **zwanzig durch fünf (ist) gleich vier**, *twenty divided by five equals (is) four*
> **drei hoch zwei (ist) gleich neun**, *three squared equals (is) nine*
> **sieben Prozent**, *seven per cent*

NUMERICAL COMPOUNDS

> ■ **einfach**, *simple*
> **zweifach**, *double* (also **doppelt**)
> **dreifach**, *triple*, etc.

These are ordinary adjectives.

- **einmal**, *once*
  zweimal, *twice*
  dreimal, *three times*, etc.
  x-mal, zigmal, *umpteen times*

- **erstens**, *firstly*
  zweitens, *secondly*
  drittens, *thirdly*, etc.

- **einerlei**, *one kind of* (also: *the same kind of; identical*)
  zweierlei, *two kinds of*
  dreierlei, *three kinds of*, etc.

These are invariable adjectives.

Note the idiomatic use of **einerlei**:

> **es ist mir einerlei**, *it's all the same to me*

TIME AND DATE

Time of day

> **wie spät ist es?; wieviel Uhr ist es?**, *what time is it?*
>
> **haben Sie die richtige Uhrzeit bitte?**, *do you have the right time please?* (more polite)

es ist ein Uhr, one o'clock
- **fünf (Minuten) nach eins**, *five past one*
- **Viertel nach eins**, *quarter past one*
- **fünfundzwanzig (Minuten) nach eins / fünf vor halb zwei**, *twenty-five past one*
- **halb zwei**, *half past one* (NB: not '*half past two*'!)
- **Viertel vor zwei**, *quarter to two*
- **eine Minute vor zwei**, *a minute to two*
- **zwei Uhr**, *two o'clock*
- **fünf vor (nach) zwölf**, *five to (past) twelve*

> **Mittag**, *twelve noon*
> **Mitternacht**, *midnight*

The forms **Viertel (auf) drei** and **drei Viertel (auf) drei** for *quarter past two* and *quarter to three* (etc.) are sometimes heard in south Germany, constructed on the same look-ahead principle as **halb drei**.

■ There are no equivalents to a.m. and p.m. in German. To be specific use:

> **vormittags**, *in the morning*
> **nachmittags**, *in the afternoon*
> **abends**, *in the evening*
> **nachts**, *at night*

■ Units of clock time

> **die Sekunde**, *second*
> **die Minute**, *minute*
> **die Stunde**, *hour*
> **eine halbe Stunde**, *half an hour*
> **eine Viertelstunde**, *a quarter of an hour,*
> **eine Dreiviertelstunde**, *three-quarters of an hour*

The 24-hour clock

The 24-hour clock is much more common in Germany than here, being used for virtually all official and semi-official times; the 12-hour clock is standard in conversation, however.

> **es ist ein Uhr fünfzehn**, *01.15*
> **ein Uhr dreißig**, *01.30*
> **ein Uhr fünfundvierzig**, *01.45*
> **dreizehn Uhr**, *13.00*
> **vierundzwanzig Uhr**, *24.00* (24 as opposed to 00 is only normally used for midnight exactly)
> **null Uhr eins**, *00.01*

Expressions with time of day

- **ab**, *from*

    ab sieben Uhr, *from seven (on)*

- **bis**, *by*

    bis elf Uhr sind wir da, *we'll be there by eleven*

    Bis also means *until*—the context makes clear which:

    das Restaurant hat von Mittag bis drei auf, *the restaurant's open from twelve to three*

See Prepositions, pp. 169–70.

- **gegen; ungefähr um**, *at about*

    der Zug kommt ungefähr um Mittag (gegen Mittag) an, *the train comes in at about 12 o'clock*

    Ungefähr um is to be preferred, since **gegen** is ambiguous—it could mean '*towards*', i.e. *just before* (clearer: **kurz vor**). **Um . . . herum**, *about*, is also common in spoken German.

- **Punkt; genau; gerade**, *exactly*

    es ist Punkt/genau/gerade eins, *it's exactly one o'clock*

    es ist genau/gerade ein Uhr zwanzig, *it's exactly twenty past one*

    es ist genau halb, *it's exactly half past*

- **um**, *at*

    um wieviel Uhr fährt der Zug?, *what time does the train go?*

    um sieben Uhr, *at seven o'clock*

Note also: **Schlag zwei**, *on (at) the stroke of two.*

- **vorbei**, *past*

    es ist Mitternacht vorbei, *it's past midnight*

Note the position of **vorbei**.

Days, months, seasons

- **Sonntag**, *Sunday*
  Montag, *Monday*
  Dienstag, *Tuesday*
  Mittwoch, *Wednesday*
  Donnerstag, *Thursday*
  Freitag, *Friday*
  Sonnabend (north Germany), **Samstag** (south Germany), *Saturday*

Days of the week are masculine.

> **was ist heute für ein Tag?—Heute ist Montag**, *what day is it?—It's Monday*

- **Januar**, *January*
  Februar, *February*
  März, *March*
  April, *April*
  Mai, *May*
  Juni, *June*
  Juli, *July*
  August, *August*
  September, *September*
  Oktober, *October*
  November, *November*
  Dezember, *December*

Months are masculine.

- **der Frühling**, *spring*
  der Sommer, *summer*
  der Herbst, *autumn*
  der Winter, *winter*

Seasons are normally used with the definite article.

- **vorgestern**, *the day before yesterday*
  gestern, *yesterday*

heute, *today*
morgen, *tomorrow*
übermorgen, *the day after tomorrow*

■ **gestern morgen, gestern früh,** *yesterday morning*
gestern nachmittag, *yesterday afternoon*
gestern abend, *last night (= yesterday evening)*

heute nacht, *last night (= during the night)*
heute früh, heute morgen, heute vormittag, *this morning*
heute nachmittag, heute mittag, *this afternoon*
heute abend, *tonight (= this evening)*
heute nacht, *tonight (= during the night)*

morgen früh, *tomorrow morning (tomorrow early is* **morgen ganz früh**)
morgen nachmittag, *tomorrow afternoon*
morgen abend, *tomorrow evening*

Note the ambiguity in **heute nacht,** *last night* or *tonight*. The context makes the meaning clear.

■ **vor drei Monaten,** *three months ago*
vorletzte Woche, *the week before last*
gestern vor einer Woche, gestern vor acht (NB!) Tagen, *a week ago yesterday*
heute in einer Woche, heute über acht Tage, *a week today*
übernächste Woche, *the week after next*
in drei Monaten, *in three months time*

■ **lange vorher,** *long before*
ein Jahr vorher, *a year before*
am Tag vorher, tags zuvor, *the day before*
am folgenden Tag, tags darauf, *the day after*
ein Jahr danach, *a year after*
lange danach, *long after*

The date

> **der wievielte ist heute?, den wievielten haben wir heute?**, *what's the date today?*
>
> **heute ist der erste Januar**, *today's the first of January*
>
> **heute ist der Erste**, *today's the first*
>
> **wir fahren Sonnabend den Sechsten**, *we go on Saturday the sixth*

Length of time

■ **lang(e)**, *for* (time completed, normally in the past)

> **wie lange war er dort?**, *how long was he there?*
>
> **er war drei Wochen (lang) dort**, *he was there (for) three weeks*
>
> **er war stundenlang (tagelang, wochenlang**, etc.) **dort**, *he was there (for) hours (days, weeks, etc.)*

Lang(e) may be omitted, except in the question and where it forms part of the word. The **-e** is often dropped. Note **eine Zeitlang**, *for a time*.

■ **auf, für**, *for* (time intended)

> **(auf) wie lange ist er hier?**, *how long is he here (for)?*
>
> **er ist auf drei Wochen hier**, *he's here for three weeks*

Though this construction normally refers to future time, it can be set back into the past, still conveying the intention:

> **er war auf drei Wochen dort**, *he was there for three weeks (he intended to stay that long)*

Auf is followed by the accusative. **Für** may be used instead of **auf**. It is slightly less common.

■ **seit,** *for* (time started in the past, continuing into the present)

> **seit wie lange ist er hier?**, *how long has he been here?*
>
> **er ist hier seit drei Wochen**, *he's been here for three weeks*

▶ For tenses with **seit** see p. 179.

Definite time expressions

Definite expressions of time stand in the accusative, or take a preposition, usually **an** or **in** + dative:

> **den ganzen Tag (Morgen, Nachmittag,** etc.), *all day (morning, afternoon,* etc.)
>
> **jeden Tag**, *every day*
>
> **alle drei Tage**, *every third day*
>
> **diesen Freitag, dieses Jahr**, *this Friday, this year*
>
> **nächsten Freitag**, *next Friday* (= the coming Friday)
>
> **den nächsten Tag, am nächsten Tag**, *next day* (= the day following)
>
> **am Freitag**, *on Friday*
>
> **im Januar**, *in January*
>
> **im Frühling**, *in spring*
>
> **am Abend**, *in the evening*
>
> **am Tag**, *by day*
>
> **dreimal am Tag (in der Woche)**, *three times a day (a week)*
>
> **in der Nacht**, *by night, in the night*
>
> **im Jahre 1999**, *in 1999* (or just **1999**—but NOT '**in 1999**')
>
> **im siebzehnten Jahrhundert**, *in the 17th century*
>
> **n. Chr. (= nach Christus)**, *AD*
>
> **v. Chr. (= vor Christus)**, *BC*

Folgend, *following,* **letzt,** *last,* **vorig, vergangen,** *previous,* may be used in the same way as **nächst.**

No preposition is used with **Anfang, Mitte, Ende:**

> **er kommt Anfang (Mitte, Ende) Mai,** *he's coming at the beginning (in the middle, at the end) of May*

Indefinite time expressions

Indefinite expressions of time stand in the genitive:

> **eines Tages,** *one day*
> **eines Abends,** *one evening*
> **eines Montags,** *one Monday*
> **morgens, vormittags,** *in the morning*
> **nachmittags,** *in the afternoon*
> **abends,** *in the evening*
> **wochentags,** *on weekdays*
> **sonntags,** *on Sundays*

By analogy: **eines Nachts,** *one night,* **nachts,** *at night*—in spite of the fact that **Nacht** is feminine!

MEASUREMENTS

> **welche Maße hat die Küche?,** *what are the kitchen's measurements?*
> **die Küche ist 3,20 Meter (drei Meter zwanzig, or—more technically—dreikommazweinull Meter) lang, 2,10 Meter breit und 2,20 Meter hoch,** *the kitchen is 3·2 metres long, 2·1 metres wide, and 2·2 metres high*
> **3,20 (Meter) mal 2,10 mal 2,20,** *3·2 metres by 2·1 by 2·2*
> **welche Größe haben Sie (tragen Sie)?,** *what size are you (do you take)?*
> **ich habe (trage) Größe 13,** *I'm (I take) size 13*
> **wieviel wiegst du?,** *what do you weigh?*
> **ich wiege einhundertdreißig Kilo,** *I weigh 130 kg.*

wie groß sind Sie?, *how tall are you?*

ich bin ein Meter neunzig groß, *I'm 1·9 metres tall*

drei Meter tief, drei Meter dick, *three metres deep,
three metres thick*

das Thermometer steht auf zwei (Grad), *the
thermometer is at (on) two degrees*

2000 cm³ (zweitausend Kubikzentimeter), *2000 cc*

| Word Order

WORD ORDER IN MAIN CLAUSES

There are two types of word order in main clauses in German, *normal order*, in which the subject comes first, the verb second, and then the rest of the clause third; and *inverted order*, in which something other than the subject comes first, the verb second, the subject (usually) third, and then the rest of the clause fourth.

Normal and inverted order

■ In both normal and inverted order the verb is firmly fixed as the second grammatical element in the clause. Subject, object, adverb, or adverb clause may precede the verb in a German sentence, but only one of these.

☐ Normal order, subject first, verb second:

> **der junge Mann stand um halb neun sehr böse vorm Kino**, *the young man was standing outside the cinema at half past eight in a very bad temper*

☐ Inverted order, verb second, subject third:

> **furchtbar böse stand der junge Mann um halb neun vorm Kino**
> **um halb neun stand der junge Mann furchtbar böse vorm Kino**
> **vorm Kino stand der junge Mann um halb neun furchtbar böse**

In each of these instances the verb is the second grammatical element in the sentence; in each instance one (and only one!) adverb phrase stands in front of it and the subject stands after it.

The first element in inverted order may be an entire subordinate clause (itself in subordinate order, see p. 222); it will be followed by a comma, with the main-clause subject next and then the main-clause subject:

> **wenn du so spät ankommst** (subordinate clause),
> **bin** (main-clause verb) **ich** (main-clause subject)
> **natürlich böse**, *if you arrive so late naturally I'm
> cross*

■ A coordinating conjunction may introduce a second or subsequent main clause to the sentence, followed by normal order:

> **er war furchtbar böse, denn der Film hatte
> schon angefangen**, *he was in a very bad temper,
> for the film had already started*

The coordinating conjunction **denn** (see p. 195) is here followed by normal order: subject, verb, rest of sentence.

■ There may be two or more main clauses joined by **und** or **oder** where, as in English, the subject is understood from the first:

> **er lief ins Wohnzimmer, nahm seinen Rechner in
> die Hand und lief wieder hinaus**, *he ran into the
> living room, picked up his calculator, and ran out again*

This is in fact normal order: the **er** from the first **er lief** is understood before **nahm** and again before the second **lief**.

In German the subject can be understood *only* in its normal position in front of the verb. If there is something else standing in front of the verb in the second or third clause of a sentence like the one above, the subject, in this case **er**, must be expressed:

> **er lief ins Wohnzimmer, nahm seinen Rechner in
> die Hand, und ohne weiteres lief er hinaus**,
> *. . . and without further ado ran out* (in German the
> subject **er** must be there if **ohne weiteres** stands
> before the verb)

■ The following, standing at the head of a clause, are not felt to be part of it; they have a comma after them and do not affect subsequent word order:

□ **ja** and **nein**

> **nein, das glaube ich nicht,** *no, I don't believe it*

□ exclamations (which may have either a comma or an exclamation mark)

> **ach, ich habe meinen Schlüssel vergessen,** *oh, I've forgotten my key*

□ names of people addressed

> **Günter, dich meinte ich nicht,** *Günter, I didn't mean you*

□ **er sagte,** and other verbs introducing indirect speech, but not followed by **daß:**

> **er sagte, er wollte sofort bezahlen,** *he said he wanted to pay right away*

See p. 42.

□ summing-up expressions, for example

> **das heißt,** *that is*
> **im Gegenteil,** *on the contrary*
> **ehrlich gesagt,** *to be honest*
> **unter uns,** *between ourselves*
> **wie gesagt,** *as I said*
> **wissen Sie,** *you know*
>
> **unter uns, ich konnte sie nie leiden,** *between ourselves, I never liked her*

Position of the parts of the verb in compound tenses

■ In past compound tenses the auxiliary verb stays in the second position, but the past participle goes to the end of the clause:

> **er hatte sehr lang gewartet**, *he had waited for a very long time*

■ With future and conditional tenses the auxiliary verb stays in second position, and the infinitive goes to the end:

> **sie wird sicher bald kommen**, *she's sure to turn up soon*

■ With future perfect and conditional perfect tenses the order at the end of the clause is past participle, then infinitive:

> **er wird sehr lange gewartet haben**, *he will have been waiting a very long time*

Position of the prefix with separable verbs

■ In simple tenses of separable verbs the separable prefix goes to the end of the clause:

> **der Film fing vor zwanzig Minuten an**, *the film started twenty minutes ago*

■ In compound tenses of such verbs the prefix and the past participle or the prefix and the infinitive both go to the end of the clause and join up:

> **der Film hat schon angefangen**, *the film has already started*
> **der Film wird bald anfangen**, *the film will soon start*

▶ See Separable Prefixes, p. 33, and Double Prefixes, pp. 34–6.

Position of the verb in direct questions

In direct questions the verb is placed either first, or, if there is a question word to introduce the question, immediately after this:

> **bleibst du noch lange hier vorm Kino stehen?**, *are you going to stay standing here in front of the cinema for much longer?*

wo bist du denn geblieben?, *where have you been, then?*

As in English a statement with the appropriate intonation may be used as a question. The verb is then second:

du kommst rein?, *(are) you coming in?*

Position of the verb in commands

In commands the verb is usually placed first in the sentence. If the subject is expressed it follows the verb:

komm schnell rein, wir verpassen den Film!,
come on in quickly, we're missing the film
sei du mal ruhig!, *(you) just be quiet!*

Position of the subject

■ In statements the subject is normally first or third, though object pronouns after the verb may displace a noun subject to fourth position:

noch lange ruhte sich der alte Großvater in der Küche aus, *for some time yet the old grandfather stayed resting in the kitchen*

Here the reflexive direct object is third, the noun subject fourth.

Putting something other than the subject first in a statement usually gives extra emphasis to whatever is put first.

zum allerletzten Mal wiederhole ich die Frage,
I shall repeat the question for the very last time

■ In questions the subject is second or (if there is a question word) third, immediately after the verb. As in statements, an object pronoun after the verb may stand before a noun subject.

Position of the object

■ Objects usually come early in the sentence after the verb. In normal order a pronoun object comes directly after the verb:

> **er nahm sich schnell noch etwas von dem schmackhaften Eintopf**, *he quickly helped himself to some more of the tasty stew*

The **sich** (indirect object) comes straight after the verb; the short adverb **schnell**, however, comes before the long direct object **noch etwas von dem schmackhaften Eintopf**.

■ If there is more than one object

□ pronoun objects always precede noun objects:

> **schick mir eine Karte!**, *send me a card*

□ with two pronoun objects the accusative comes first:

> **schick sie mir!**, *send it to me*

□ with two noun objects the dative comes first:

> **schick Karen die Karte!**, *send Karen the card*

This is identical with the most common (though not the only possible) order of objects in English.

Position of the complement

The complement of such verbs as **sein**, *to be*, **werden**, *to become*, and **bleiben**, *to remain*, goes as late in the clause as possible:

> **sie ist sicher dieses Jahr zum erstenmal Karnevalsprinzessin**, *she's certainly going to be carnival princess this year, for the first time*

Position of adverbs

■ The normal order of adverbs is *time—reason—manner—place*:

> **er fährt sofort mit dem Auto nach Hildesheim,**
> *he's going right away by car to Hildesheim*

> **er fährt heute wegen ihrer Heirat nach**
> **Hildesheim,** *he's going to Hildesheim today for*
> *(because of) her wedding*

If there are two adverbs of the same kind the more general one comes first:

> **er fuhr letztes Jahr am einundzwanzigsten**
> **August nach Hildesheim,** *last year he went to*
> *Hildesheim, on the twenty-first of August*

A time adverb will often precede a noun object:

> **er hat gestern sein Auto verkauft,** *he sold his car*
> *yesterday*

The order and position of adverbs is, however, far from rigid: moving one to a position late in the sentence gives it additional importance:

> **er hat sein Auto gestern verkauft** (he sold it yesterday,
> he can't have sold it today, whatever you say)

Generally speaking, in German the strong, important position in the sentence is at the end.

■ Negative adverbs (**nicht, nie,** etc.) stand in front of the word or words they are negating:

> **das habe ich nie wirklich gesagt,** *I never really*
> *said that*

If they negate the action of the verb they stand as near the end as possible:

> **das habe ich wirklich nie gesagt,** *I really never said that.*

▶ See also **kein,** p. 153.

WORD ORDER IN SUBORDINATE CLAUSES

A subordinate clause may be introduced by a subordinating
conjunction (any conjunction except the six coordinating ones,
see p. 195), or by a relative pronoun (see p. 139). All parts of
the clause stay in main-clause order except the verb, which
moves to the very end of the clause.

> normal order: **ich habe nicht genug Geld**, *I haven't
> enough money*
>
> subordinate order: **ich tue es, weil ich nicht genug
> Geld habe**, *I'm doing it because I haven't enough
> money*

■ In subordinate order a separable verb recombines with its
prefix at the end of the clause:

> normal order: **ich gehe in zwanzig Minuten fort**,
> *I'm going out in twenty minutes*
>
> subordinate order: **ich tue es, weil ich in zwanzig
> Minuten fortgehe**, *I'm doing it because I'm going
> out in twenty minutes*

▶ See p. 33.

■ If there is a past participle or an infinitive at the end of the
clause the verb goes beyond these, right at the end:

> **ein Mann muß tun, was ein Mann tun muß**, *a
> man's got to do what a man's got to do*

However, if there are two or more infinitive forms at the end of the
clause the verb will stand immediately before and not after these:

> **damals hat ein Mann tun müssen, was ein Mann
> hat tun müssen**, *in those days a man had to do
> what a man had to do*

▶ See p. 67.

■ If there are two subordinate clauses joined by **und** (or **oder**
or **sondern**), the verb goes to the end in both:

> **ich tue es, weil ich fortgehen muß und nicht
> sehr viel Zeit habe**, *I'm doing it because I'm going
> out and (I) haven't got very much time*

If two subordinate clauses share the same verb, it goes at the end of the second one:

> **ich tue es, weil ich in die Stadt fahren und fürs
> Wochenende einkaufen muß**, *I'm doing it because I
> have to go into town and shop for the weekend*

■ If one subordinate clause is embedded in another, they must both have subordinate order:

> **ich frage mich, ob das Auto, das ich letzte
> Woche gekauft habe, wirklich so viel wert ist**,
> *I'm wondering if the car I bought last week is really
> worth that much*

Don't be tempted to say or write ' . . . **ist wirklich so viel wert**'.

■ Either subordinate or inverted order may be used for exclamatory clauses:

> **was für blöde Sachen er geredet hat! / was hat er
> für blöde Sachen geredet!**, *what rubbish he talked!*

■ Subordinate order is not always adhered to in spoken German: phrases tend to be added after the verb:

> **ich bin ganz sicher, daß alles klappen wird mit
> deinem Examen**, *I'm quite sure everything'll go
> well with your exam*

There is an increasing tendency for this to occur in written German as well.

INFINITIVE PHRASES

Infinitives used in a phrase go at the end of that phrase:

> **seine Hoffung, am gleichen Tag nach Mannheim
> zu fahren, ging nicht in Erfüllung**, *his hope of
> going to Mannheim the same day was not realized*

Position of infinitives without zu

■ Infinitives without **zu** are included in the clause, at the end:

> **ich muß heute fahren**, *I've got to go today*

There, they go before a past participle:

> **er hatte an diesem Tag fahren müssen**, *he had had to go on that day*

. . . before an infinitive that forms part of the future and conditional tenses:

> **ich werde heute fahren müssen**, *I'm going to have to go today*

. . . and before the verb in subordinate order:

> **ich weiß, daß du fahren mußt**, *I know you've got to go*

Position of infinitives with zu

■ Infinitives with **zu** are placed at the end of a clause. If they have other qualifications such as adverbs or objects they form a phrase of their own, marked off from the clause by a comma (see Punctuation, p. 231).

> **er versucht zu arbeiten**, *he's trying to work*
> **sie hat versucht, ihr Auto zu verkaufen**, *she's been trying to sell her car*

■ Where an infinitive depends on a separable verb the infinitive may go before or after the prefix:

> **er fing zu arbeiten an / er fing an zu arbeiten**, *he began to work*

If the infinitive is qualified it usually goes after the prefix:

> **er fing an, regelmäßig an seinem Auto zu arbeiten**, *he began to work on his car regularly*

■ In subordinate order with a verb in a simple tense, a short infinitive phrase with **zu** is enclosed within the clause:

> **ich weiß, daß sie es zu verkaufen versucht,**
> *I know she's trying to sell it*
>
> **ich weiß, daß sie ihr Auto zu verkaufen versucht,** or **. . . daß sie versucht, ihr Auto zu verkaufen,** *I know she's trying to sell her car*

A longer infinitive phrase stands outside the clause:

> **ich weiß, daß sie versucht, diesen alten, klapprigen Trabant zu verkaufen,** *I know she's trying to sell that beat-up old Trabant*

■ In subordinate order with a verb in a compound tense, the infinitive stands outside the clause:

> **ich weiß, daß sie versucht hat, es zu verkaufen,**
> *I know she's been trying to sell it*

■ Infinitives preceded by **um . . . zu**, *in order to*, **ohne . . . zu**, *without . . . -ing*, and **(an)statt zu**, *instead of . . . -ing*, are always placed outside the clause:

> **ich bin hier, um mein Auto zu verkaufen,** *I'm here (in order) to sell my car*

OTHER PHRASES ETC. NORMALLY STANDING OUTSIDE THE CLAUSE

■ Apart from infinitives with **zu** + further qualification, the following types of phrases usually stand outside the clause:

□ question tags, like **nicht wahr?**, **ja?**, **oder?** (corresponding to *isn't it?*, *aren't you?*, or *is it?*, etc.)

> **du bleibst hier, oder?**, *you're staying here—aren't you?* (open question)
> **du bleibst hier, nicht? / nicht wahr? / ja?**, *you're staying here, aren't you?* (I'm pretty sure you are)

☐ phrases beginning **wie** and **als**, forming the second part of a comparison

> **du hast es genau so schwierig gefunden wie ich**,
> *you found it just as difficult as I did (as me)*
> **nein, ich habe es viel schwieriger gefunden als
> du**, *no, I found it a lot more difficult than you (did)*

Where **als** and **wie** simply mean *as* or *like*, functioning as a sort of equals sign, the phrase they introduce does not stand outside the clause:

> **das haben sie mir als Deutscher sagen wollen?**,
> *you meant to say that to me, as a German?*
> **das kann selbst ein Dummkopf wie ich verstehen**,
> *even an idiot like me can understand that*

☐ phrases beginning **sondern** and **außer**

> **sie hat es nicht gemacht, sondern ich**, *it wasn't
> she who did it, but me (I)*
> **ich habe nichts gelesen außer einem Krimi**, *I read
> nothing except a detective story*

Sondern phrases have a comma before them (see Punctuation, pp. 229–30).

☐ **oder nicht**, and sometimes other phrases beginning **oder**

> **wird er kommen oder nicht?**, *is he going to come or not?*
> **möchtest du Erdbeeren essen oder die Torte?**, *would
> you like strawberries or the flan?*

■ A relative clause stands outside the main clause when it refers back to a noun or pronoun standing immediately before a part of the verb at the end of the clause:

> **er hat schnell das Geld genommen, das ich ihm
> angeboten habe**, *he quickly took the money I was
> offering him*

but: **das Geld, das ich ihm angeboten habe, hat er
schnell genommen**

I Punctuation and Spelling

CAPITAL LETTERS

■ All nouns and other words used as nouns have a capital letter:

> **der Mann**, *the man*
> **das Lachen**, *laughing* (verbal noun)
> **der Reisende**, *the traveller* (present participle used as noun)

■ Pronouns:

□ The polite **Sie** and its other forms (**Ihnen, Ihr**—but not the reflexive form **sich**) always have a capital.

□ **Du** and **ihr** and their other forms (**dich, dir, dein; euch, euer**) are written with a capital when writing letters.

□ **Du** (etc.) is capitalized when referring to God.

■ Adjectives made from town names by adding **-er** have a capital:

> **der Kölner Dom**, *Cologne cathedral*

■ Adjectives in geographical and other names have a capital:

> **das Rote Meer**, *the Red Sea*
> **Deutsche Bundesbahn**, *German Railways*

■ Adjectives after indefinites have a capital:

> **etwas Grünes**, *something green*

but indefinites themselves do not take a capital:

> **etwas anderes**, *something different*
> **das übrige**, *what's left*

► See p. 108.

■ Adjectives referring to countries take a small letter as adjectives, a capital as the name of the language:

> **die deutsche Sprache**, *the German language*
> **sie spricht Englisch**, *she speaks English*

but there is no capital for the language after **auf** = *in*:

> **auf englisch**, *in English*

■ A capital is frequently used in German in mid-sentence after a colon.

■ Cardinal numbers have a small letter, except **Million, Milliarde**, and sometimes **Hundert, Tausend** (see p. 202). Fractions are written with either a capital or a small letter (see pp. 204–5).

Ordinal numbers used as adjectives have small letters, but notice:

> **Friedrich der Zweite**, *Friedrich II*

■ Nouns not used as nouns have a small letter:

> **die Schuld**, *guilt*: **du bist daran schuld**, *it's your fault*
> **das Paar**, *pair*: **ein paar Sachen**, *a few things*
> **das Leid**, *sorrow*: **er tut mir leid**, *I'm sorry for him*

Das bißchen, *bit*, is now only ever used with a small letter:

> **ein bißchen Zucker**, *a little sugar*
> **kein bißchen Zucker**, *no sugar at all*
> **das klein bißchen Zucker**, *the small amount of sugar* (note the invariable **klein**)

THE COMMA

The use of commas is largely a matter of individual style in English. In German, however, commas are used according to fixed rules that must be followed.

■ Commas are used in lists to divide off items (but not before the **und** at the end):

> **er ist jung, schön, reich und gesund**, *he's young, handsome, rich, and healthy*

■ Commas are not used between two adjectives if the second is felt to form a single concept with its noun:

> **ein schöner, saftiger Schinken**, *a nice juicy ham*
> **ein schöner westfälischer Schinken**, *a nice Westphalian ham*

■ A comma is used before and/or after each subordinate clause to separate it from the main clause:

> **Ich weiß, daß er kommen wird**. *I know he'll come.*
> **Wenn er kommt, werden wir essen.** *When he comes we'll eat.*
> **Die Leute, die kommen werden, sind mir bekannt.** *The people who're coming are known to me.*

The comma comes before, not after, the subordinating conjunction.

■ Commas separate main clauses joined by **und** or **oder**:

> **Er kam, und wir aßen.** *He came and we ate.*

but not if an element of the first has to be understood in the second:

> **Er kommt und ißt.** (= **und er ißt**) *He comes and eats.*

This element is usually the subject, but not always:

> **Er ißt hier und die anderen zu Hause.** (= **und die anderen essen**) *He eats here and the others (eat) at home.*

■ Commas are always placed before the other coordinating conjunctions (**aber, sondern, denn, allein**—see p. 195), whether they introduce a clause or a phrase:

> **Ich klopfte, aber niemand antwortete**. *I knocked but no one answered.*
>
> **Es ist nicht rot, sondern weiß**. *It is not red, but white.*

■ Unlike English, German does not separate adverb phrases with commas:

> **Er stand wie immer mit Blumen vor der Tür**. *He was standing, with flowers as always, at the door.*

Adjective phrases, however, are often given commas:

> **Er betrachtete, grün vor Neid, das Auto, das ich gerade gekauft hatte**. *He looked, green with envy, at the car I had just bought.*

■ Commas are placed round appositional phrases and before a phrase beginning **und zwar**:

> **Herr Schmidt, unser neuer Chef, ist heute erschienen, und zwar um acht Uhr**. *Herr Schmidt, our new boss, turned up today, and, would you believe it, at eight o'clock.*

■ Commas are sometimes used to join two main clauses, where the equivalent English would correctly have a semicolon. This occurs particularly where the second clause begins with **trotzdem**, *in spite of that*, **unterdessen**, *meanwhile*, and **statt dessen**, *instead*:

> **Es regnet, trotzdem wollen wir wandern**. *It's raining; in spite of that we're still going walking.*

■ A comma is used where we would use a decimal point:

> **2,3** *2·3*

It is not used in large numbers, which are written with spaces where English uses commas:

> **1999 777** *1,999,777*

▶ See Numbers, p. 201.

■ Commas are used with infinitive phrases as follows.

□ An infinitive phrase consisting only of **zu** + infinitive has no comma before it:

> **Sie versucht zu singen.** *She tries to sing.*

□ One that is longer than just **zu** + infinitive usually has a comma:

> **Sie versucht, den ganzen Ring auswendig zu lernen.** *She's trying to learn the whole of the Ring by heart.*

□ There is always a comma where the infinitive is a complement after **sein**:

> **Ihr einziges Streben ist, zu singen.** *Her only aspiration is to sing.*

□ There is no comma, however long the infinitive phrase, after the verbs **brauchen**, *to need*, **haben**, *to have*, **sein**, *to be*, **scheinen**, *to seem*, and **pflegen**, *to be accustomed*:

> **Jetzt brauchst du kein einziges Wort mehr zu sagen.** *Now you don't need to say a single word more.*

THE COLON

The colon marks an amplification or explanation of what has gone before. English may use a colon or a dash for this. In German the clause following a colon very frequently starts with a capital letter:

> **Etwas muß ich aber erklären: Das Haus ist nicht zu verkaufen.** *One thing I must make clear, however—the house is not for sale.*

The colon is also used to introduce direct speech after a verb of saying:

Sie sagte: „Komm gut nach Hause!" *She said,
'Get home safely.'*

THE HYPHEN

A hyphen is used to represent part of a compound, to avoid
clumsy repetition:

**Radio- und Fernsehgeräte (= Radiogeräte und
Fernsehgeräte)**, *radio and television sets*

It is also occasionally used, for clarity, to break up very long
compound words.

THE DASH

This usually indicates a pause, often for thought (*dash* = **der
Gedankenstrich**). It may also be used instead of three dots to
suspend the sense. It is sometimes used to separate two
passages of direct speech within the same paragraph.

INVERTED COMMAS

The opening set of inverted commas is placed on the line in
German. Both sets are printed the opposite way round from
English. German uses double inverted commas for direct
speech, whereas English more and more frequently uses single:

„Das ist nicht wahr", sagte er. *'That's not true', he
said.*

French guillemets (also printed the 'wrong' way round) are
sometimes found:

»Das ist nicht wahr!«

For speech within speech single inverted commas are used: **, '**.

THE EXCLAMATION MARK

The exclamation mark is used much more than in English. In none of the following cases is it obligatory, however. It is very frequently used . . .

- after exclamations

    Au! Das kann nicht sein! *Oh, that can't be true!*

- after imperatives

    Steh auf! *Stand up.*

- in public notices and admonitions, where English would not punctuate at all

    Das Betreten der Baustelle ist verboten! *Keep out*
    Nicht hinauslehnen! *Do not lean out of the window*

- sometimes at the start of letters, where English uses a comma

    Liebe Gisela! *Dear Gisela,*
    Sehr geehrte Damen und Herren! *Dear Sir or Madam,*

A comma is nowadays more common in German in this case.

FULL STOP

The full stop is used to end a sentence, and to indicate abbreviations. However, it is only used for abbreviations if what is normally said aloud for that abbreviation is the words for which it stands, not the letters of the abbreviation:

      d.h. (spoken: **das heißt**), *i.e.*

but: **DB** (= **Deutsche Bundesbahn**, *German Railways*)
       PKW (sometimes **Pkw;** = **Personenkraftwagen**, *passenger vehicle; car*)

Notice that **usw.** (= **und so weiter**, *etc.*) has only one full stop.

A full stop is used to abbreviate an ordinal number (including its adjective ending):

> **am 20. August (am zwanzigsten August)**, *on the 20th of August*

EMPHASIS

In older printed material this is shown by spaced printing:

> **Ich möchte d e n** . *I want that one.*

This has now been largely replaced by italics, as in English:

> **Ich möchte *den*.**

SPELLING PECULIARITIES

■ Syllable division

In German a word broken at the end of a line divides according to syllables: **kom-for-ta-bel**, *com-fort-able*. This is, however, largely a matter for printers, since we almost never split a word when writing by hand. Beware, though, of the fact that the letters **ck** divide as **k-k**, so split over two lines **Zucker** becomes **Zuk- ker**, **Bäcker** becomes **Bäk- ker**.

■ Triple consonants

In compound nouns with a sequence of three identical consonants one of the three is dropped, except

☐ if the word is split between two lines:

> **das Bettuch**, *sheet*, but **Bett- tuch**

☐ if a further consonant follows:

> **fetttriefend**, *dripping with fat*

☐ if the first two of three **s**'s are written **ß**:

> **die Fußsohle**, *sole*

■ ß

The use of ß is purely a written distinction: even though it is sometimes called **'das scharfe S'**, there is *no* difference in pronunciation between ß and **ss**.

ß is used

□ always before another consonant:

> **ich mußte**, *I had to*

□ always at the end of a word, and at the end of a word contained within a compound:

> **der Schluß**, *end;* **der Schlußsatz**, *final sentence*

□ in other places, after a long vowel:

> **die Füße**, *feet* (long **ü**)
>
> but: **die Flüsse**, *rivers* (short **ü**)

With proper names usage varies and has to learned individually (the musicians, for instance, are Johann Strauß and Richard Strauss).

If ß is not available (e.g. on a keyboard) use **ss**; **sz** used for ß is old-fashioned. ß has no capital form—where a word is printed entirely in capitals **SS** is used. In Switzerland ß is often not used at all (the up-market **Neue Zürcher Zeitung** always uses **ss** only).

I Translation Problems

The following list is alphabetical. It includes items not treated in the body of the grammar, or treated in a number of different places and more conveniently brought together here. Reference is made throughout to the places in the body of the grammar where more detail may be found.

Translation problems not covered here should be tackled via the Index, or via the various alphabetical lists in the Grammar:

prepositions (German), p. 163
            (English), p. 188
adverbial particles,   p. 122
conjunctions,   p. 197
verb constructions,   p. 53.

AS

■ As a conjunction expressing time (= *when*) *as* is **wie** or **indem**. **Wie** is the more colloquial; **indem** is only used where both actions occur literally at the same time:

> **wie ich aus dem Bus stieg, begegnete ich ihr vorm Rathaus**, *as (when) I got off the bus I ran into her in front of the town hall*
> **wie/indem ich aus dem Bus stieg, verrenkte ich mir den Fuß**, *as I got off the bus I twisted my ankle*

■ As a conjunction expressing manner (= *like*) *as* must be **wie**:

> **wie Sie sehen, habe ich mir den Fuß verrenkt**, *as you see, I've sprained my ankle*

■ In comparisons of equality (*as . . . as*), the first *as* is **so**, the second **wie**:

er ist genauso unsicher wie ich, *he's just as unsure as I (am)*

The negative of this construction is **nicht so . . . wie**, *not as . . . as*:

er ist nicht so unsicher wie ich, *he's not as unsure as I (am)*

As can also be a conjunction introducing a complete clause in a comparison of equality; it is still **wie**:

sie macht es fast so gut, wie ich es gemacht habe, *she does it almost as well as I did it*

■ As a conjunction expressing cause (= *since*), *as* is **da**:

da er nicht hier ist, werde ich es selber machen, *as he's not here I'll do it myself*

■ Meaning '*in the capacity of*', *as* is **als**:

ich als Fachmann kann Ihnen versichern, daß . . . , *I, as an expert, can assure you that . . .*

▶ *As if* is **als ob** or **als wenn**. See p. 44.

FOR

■ Conjunction, **denn**:

du mußt es tun, denn wir werden sonst keine Gelegenheit finden, *you must do it, for we shan't find any opportunity otherwise*

Denn is slightly less formal than *for* is in English. As in English the **denn** *(for)* clause can't start the sentence.

■ Preposition with time (for other prepositional uses of *for* consult pp. 190–1):

□ A completed period in the past— **lang**, or a time expression in the accusative:

er war drei Jahre lang im Jemen, *he was in the Yemen for three years*

er mußte einen ganzen Monat warten, *he had to wait for a whole month*

☐ A period starting in the present or the future— **auf** + ACC or **für**:

ich bin auf/für drei Wochen hier, *I'm here for three weeks*

☐ An intended period in the past— **auf** + ACC or **für**:

sie kam auf/für drei Jahre nach Deutschland, *she came to Germany for three years* (no statement of how long she stayed)

☐ A period in the past stretching up to the present— **seit** + present tense:

sie ist seit drei Wochen hier, *she's been here for three weeks*

▶ See pp. 178–9 for tenses used.

☐ A period in the distant past stretching up to the point in the past that we are speaking of— **seit** + past tense:

er war seit drei Jahren im Jemen, als . . . , *he had been in the Yemen for three years, when . . .*

▶ See pp. 178–9 for tenses used.

IF

■ *If* introducing a clause of possibility is **wenn**:

wenn du kommst, bring es mit, *if you come bring it with you*

It may also introduce a shortened version of this kind of clause:

wenn überhaupt, *if at all*
wenn möglich, *if possible*

■ Introducing an indirect question, *if* (*= whether*) is **ob**:

> **ich weiß nicht, ob ich es mitbringen kann,** *I don't know if I can bring it with me*

-ING

The *-ing* form of the verb in English corresponds basically to the present participle in German (see pp. 36–7), but it is used in ways in English that are not always paralleled in German.

■ There is no German equivalent to the English continuous tenses (*I am waiting*, etc.). The equivalent simple or compound tense must be used:

> **ich esse,** *I'm eating*
> **ich aß,** *I was eating*
> **ich habe gegessen,** *I have been eating*

■ When two actions are going on at the same time, the *-ing* phrase is translated by a clause introduced by **indem**:

> **indem sie auf das Auto wartete, dachte sie an Hans,** *waiting for the car she thought of Hans*

Auf das Auto wartend, dachte sie . . . is not impossible, but much rarer than in English.

■ When two actions occur consecutively, the *-ing* phrase is translated by a second main clause:

> **er machte die Tür auf und stieg aus dem Auto,** *opening the door, he got out of the car*

■ Where the English present participle is used as a noun, German uses a verbal noun (the infinitive with a capital letter):

> **Warten is so langweilig,** *waiting is so boring*
> **wir haben keine Zeit zum Tennisspielen,** *we've no time for playing tennis*

■ When the English *-ing* form is the equivalent of *to* + infinitive, **zu** + infinitive is used in German:

> **sie begann zu weinen**, *she began crying (= began to cry)*
>
> **danach zu schicken, wäre das einfachste**, *sending for it (= to send for it) would be easiest*

■ With the verbs *to see*, *to hear*, *to feel* (and many others) English can make a present participle depend on the object (*I hear her returning*). A similar construction is possible in German with **hören**, **sehen**, and a limited number of other verbs; in German a dependent infinitive without **zu** is used:

> **ich höre sie zurückkommen**, *I hear her returning*

► See pp. 46–7.

■ *Instead of* + *-ing* and *without* + *-ing* are translated by **anstatt**, *instead of*, and **ohne**, *without*, + **zu** + infinitive:

> **ohne zu sprechen**, *without speaking*
>
> **anstatt radzufahren**, *instead of cycling*

■ *By . . . -ing* is translated as **indem** + clause or **dadurch, daß** + clause:

> **er ist uns entkommen, indem er ein Motorboot gestohlen hat / er ist uns dadurch entkommen, daß er ein Motorboot gestohlen hat**, *he got away from us by stealing a motorboat*

A similar construction to **dadurch, daß** is used when a verb that takes a preposition is followed by *-ing*:

bestehen auf, *to insist on*

> **ich bestehe darauf, daß ich mitkomme**, *I insist on coming with you*
>
> **ich bestehe darauf, daß er mitkommt**, *I insist on him coming with you*

► See pp. 52–3.

ONLY

■ As an adjective after an article, **einzig**:

> **das ist das einzige Geschenk, das ich bekommen habe**, *it's the only present I got*

■ As an adjective before an article, **nur**:

> **nur das Baby war da**, *only the baby was there*

■ Before a pronoun, **allein** or **nur**. Allein follows its pronoun, **nur** precedes it:

> **sie allein war da / nur sie war da**, *only she was there*

■ As a time adverb, **erst**:

> **erst als sie die Tür aufmachte**, *only when she opened the door*
> **erst nach dem Abendessen**, *only after supper*
> **erst jetzt verstehe ich**, *only now do I understand*
> **die Bank macht erst um zehn auf**, *the bank only opens at ten*

▶ For **erst als/wenn**, *only when*, see Until, p. 249.

■ Otherwise, as an adverb, *only* is **nur**:

> **nur langsam machte sie die Tür auf**, *she opened the door only slowly*
> **wenn sie das nur früher gesagt hätte**, *if only she had said that earlier*

■ As a conjunction, *only* is **allein** or **aber**:

> **ich hätte es getan, allein/aber ich wollte nicht**, *I'd have done it, only I didn't want to*

▶ *Not only . . . but also* is **nicht nur . . . sondern auch**. See p. 194.

PUT

The translation of the verb *to put* depends on the position in which whatever is 'put' finally ends up.

- **stellen** *(to place)*: the object stands in a vertical position

  stellen Sie die Flaschen dorthin, *put the bottles down there*

- **legen** *(to lay)*: the object lies horizontally

  legen Sie die Platte dorthin, *put the disc down there*

- **stecken** *(to stick)*: the object is put into something

  stecken Sie den Brief in den Kasten, *put the letter into the letterbox*

- **setzen** *(to set)*: the object is put into a sitting position; this is also the verb used for many non-literal meanings of *put*

  er setzte ihr das Baby auf den Schoß, *he put the baby on her lap*

  setzen Sie ihren Namen dort, bitte, *put your name there please*

  man hat den Lift außer Betrieb gesetzt, *they've put the lift out of action*

- **Tun**, *to do*, is much used in the spoken (but not the written) language for all senses of *to put*:

  tun Sie sie dorthin, *put them down there*

  Observe the difference between **legen**, *to lay* = *to put into a lying position*, and the strong verb **liegen**, *to lie* = *to be in a lying position*. Similarly, **setzen**, *to set* = *to put into a sitting position*, and **sitzen** (strong), *to sit* = *to be in a sitting position*.

SINCE

- Preposition indicating time: **seit**

  seit Sonntag, *since Sunday*

er ist seit letzter Woche hier, *he's been here since last week*

▶ For tense with **seit**, preposition, see pp. 178–9.

■ Conjunction indicating time: **seitdem** or **seit**

seitdem er hier ist, habe ich nur Ärger mit ihm, *since he's been here I've been having nothing but trouble with him*

▶ For tenses with **seit(dem)**, see pp. 199–200.

■ Conjunction indicating reason: **da**

da er aber hier ist, muß ich mich irgendwie damit abfinden, *since he's here, though, I'll have to put up with it somehow*

SO

■ **So** translated **so**:

☐ = *to such a degree*

ich bin so müde, daß ich nicht mehr gehen kann, *I'm so tired (that) I can't walk any further*

☐ = *therefore*

er war nicht da, so mußte ich allein gehen, *he wasn't there, so I had to go alone*

☐ = *thus*

so hätte man eigentlich gedacht, *so one might in fact have thought*

☐ before an adjective (note the position of the article in German)

nach einer so langen Reise, *after so long a journey*

☐ in a negative comparison

sie ist nicht so alt wie ich, *she's not so old as I (am)*

■ *So* translated **also**:

☐ = *for that reason*

morgen hab' ich Geburtstag, also mußt du dich darauf vorbereiten, *tomorrow's my birthday, so you must get ready for it*

☐ summing up (= *then*)

das ist es also, *so that's it*

■ *So* as object of verb: **es**

ich hätte es gesagt, wenn . . . *I'd have said so, if . . .*

The **es** must come after the verb. If you wish to invert, use **das**:

das hat er sehr langsam getan, *he did so very slowly*

Verbs of thinking and hoping have nothing at all:

ja, ich denke, *yes, I think so*

■ *So much the* + adjective: **um so** + adjective:

um so besser, *so much the better*

■ *So as to:* **um . . . zu**

du solltest laufen, um nicht kalt zu werden, *you should run so as not to get cold*

■ *Something so* + adjective: **so etwas** + adjectival noun

so etwas Schönes, *something so beautiful*

SO THAT

So that is **damit** or **so daß**.

■ **Damit** means '*with the intention that*':

> **ich habe den Regenschirm mitgebracht, damit
> du trocken bleibst,** *I've brought the umbrella, so
> that you'll stay dry*

In literary German the subjunctive is sometimes found after **damit**.

■ **So daß** means '*with the result that*':

> **es hat furchtbar geregnet, so daß ich den
> Regenschirm aufspannen mußte,** *it rained
> dreadfully, so (that) I had to put the umbrella up*

As in English, the *so* can move into the main clause:

> **es hat so furchtbar geregnet, daß ich den
> Regenschirm aufspannen mußte,** *it rained so
> dreadfully that I had to put the umbrella up*

THAT

That has four different grammatical uses in English, each
translated differently into German.

■ It may be a demonstrative pronoun:

> **gib mir das dort,** *give me that*
> **das ist aber schön!,** *that's really nice*

Dies(es) could equally be used, or less commonly **jenes**. See
pp. 137–8 for more detail.

■ It may be a demonstrative adjective:

> **ich hätte gern *den* Kuchen, bitte,** *I should like that
> cake please*

Diesen Kuchen could equally be used, or less commonly
jenen Kuchen. See p. 115 for more detail.

■ It may be a relative pronoun:

> **das Geschenk, das du mitgebracht hast,** *the
> present that you brought*
> **der Mann, den ich geschickt habe,** *the man that I sent*

Welches, welchen would also be possible. See pp. 139–40 for more detail.

■ It may be a conjunction:

> **ich weiß, daß es nicht sehr leicht ist**, *I know that it's not very easy*

This is **daß**, with subordinate order.

Don't confuse **ich weiß, daß . . .** with **das Geschenk, das . . . .** Daß introduces a noun clause, here the object of **ich weiß**, telling us what 'I know'—**daß** is a conjunction. **Das** introduces an adjective clause, telling us more about a specific noun, here **das Geschenk**, *the present*. **Das** is neuter because **das Geschenk** is neuter—**das** is a relative pronoun.

THERE

There in German is either **da** or **dort**. **Dort** indicates a quite precise place, **da** is more general:

> **da ist jemand**, *there's somebody there*
> **er ist dort auf der Terrasse**, *he's there on the terrace*

■ *There* with a motion verb

There used with a motion verb must be **dahin** or **dorthin**, *to there*:

> **ich fahre morgen dahin**, *I'm going there tomorrow*

With other adverbs of place German makes a similar distinction between 'motion towards' and 'no motion towards', by using **nach**:

> **ich bin unten**, *I'm downstairs*
> **kommen Sie nach unten**, *come downstairs*

▶ See pp. 119–20.

■ *There is, there are*

There is, there are in German is **es ist, es sind**. Very often, however, German prefers a more specific verb like **es steht**, *there stands*, **es liegt**, *there lies*. These agree, as **sein** does, with the noun in the nominative that stands after them, and not with the **es**, producing the odd-looking plurals **es stehen**, *there stand*, **es liegen**, *there lie*, etc.

When existence rather than position is being spoken of **es gibt** + accusative is used for *there is, there are*. The verb stays in the singular:

> **es gibt viele Leute, die das sagen**, *there are a lot of people who say that*

▶ See pp. 72–3.

TO LIKE

The basic translation of *to like* is **gern haben** ('*to have gladly*'):

> **hast du Kinder gern?**, *do you like children?*
> **ich hätte gern zwei Stück Kuchen**, *I should like two pieces of cake*

■ Where English follows *to like* with the *-ing* form of the verb, German uses that verb + **gern**:

> **fährst du gern Ski?**, *do you like skiing?*

Especially with verbs of eating and drinking, but also with other verbs, German uses this construction where English simply uses *to like* + object:

> **sie trinkt gern Milch**, *she likes milk*
> **ißt du gern Kartoffelsalat?**, *do you like potato ~~s~~ ad?*
> **ich höre gern Brahms**, *I like Brahms*

■ The impersonal verb **es gefällt mir** indicates an immediate rather than a lasting impression:

> **das Bild? Ja, es gefällt mir**, *that picture? Yes, I like it*

■ **Mögen** also means *to like* (amongst other things); the present tense is used particularly for people:

> **ich mag sie nicht so sehr**, *I don't like her all that much*

This construction is more common in the negative.

The past subjunctive, **möchte**, *would like*, used as a conditional, is very common indeed:

> **ich möchte noch Kaffee, bitte**, *I should like some more coffee, please*
>
> **möchten Sie was kaufen?**, *would you like (do you want) to buy something?*

Gern may be added to **möchte** with little if any change to the meaning. **Ich möchte gern** is particularly used when buying things in shops:

> **ich möchte gern drei Pfund Pflaumen, bitte**, *I should like three pounds of plums please*

▶ See p. 119 for the position of **gern** in the sentence, and further details.

▶ For **mögen** see pp. 62–3.

UNTIL

■ Preposition, followed by an adverb or an adverbial phrase— **bis**:

> **bis drei Uhr**, *until three o'clock*
>
> **bis morgen**, *until tomorrow (see you tomorrow)*

■ Preposition, followed by a noun or pronoun— **bis** + second preposition, usually **zu**:

> **bis zum Letzten des Monats**, *until the last of the month*
>
> **bis auf weiteres**, *until futher notice*

- Negative preposition, *not until*— **erst** (*only*) + a preposition:

  > **erst am Letzten des Monats**, *not until (only on) the last of the month*
  >
  > **erst um Mitternacht**, *not until midnight*
  >
  > **erst nach dem Krieg**, *not until after the war*

- Conjunction— **bis**:

  > **bis es repariert wird, müssen Sie irgendwie ohne auskommen**, *until it's repaired you must manage without it somehow*

- Negative conjunction, *not until*— **erst als, erst wenn**:

  > **erst wenn sie es erklären**, *not until they explain it*
  >
  > **erst als sie es erklärt hatten**, *not until they'd explained it*

The difference between **erst wenn** and **erst als** is the same as that between the simple conjunctions **wenn** and **als** (see p. 197).

▶ See also **bis**, pp. 198–9.

WHEN

- *When* in German as a question word is **wann**. This is used in both direct and indirect questions:

  > **wann kommt sie zurück?**, *when is she coming back?*
  >
  > **ich weiß nicht, wann sie zurückkommt**, *I don't know when she's coming back*

- *When* as a conjunction, referring to one occasion in the past, is **als**:

  > **ich war da, als sie zurückkam**, *I was there when she came back*

Referring to the present, the future, or to more than one occasion in the past, it is **wenn**:

ich war jedesmal da, wenn sie zurückkam, *I was always there when she came back*

- **Wo** is frequently used for when after expressions of time:

    am Tag, wo sie zurückkam, war ich da, *I was there on the day when she came back*

▶ See pp. 197–8 for more detail.

WHICH

Which is both a question word (referring to both people and things) and a relative (referring to things).

- In questions, as an adjective used with a noun it is **welcher**:

    welche Sorte möchten Sie?, *which kind would you like?*

Similarly in indirect questions:

    ich weiß nicht, welche Sorte ich möchte, *I don't know which kind I want*

▶ See p. 116–17.

- As a pronoun in questions it is **welcher**:

    welches? Das dort im Schaufenster, *which? That one in the window*

▶ See p. 144.

- As a relative pronoun it is **der** or **welcher**:

    das Sofa, auf dem (auf welchem) du sitzt, *the sofa which you're sitting on*

▶ See pp. 139–42.

Glossary of Grammatical Terms

Abstract Noun The name of something that is not a concrete object or person. Words such as *difficulty, hope, discussion* are abstract nouns.

Accusative The direct object case in German. See Case.

Active See Passive.

Adjectival Noun An adjective used as if it were a noun: *the good, the bad, and the really horrid.* are adjectives used as nouns (with the definite article *the*).

Adjective A word describing a noun. *A big, blue, untidy painting*— *big, blue, untidy* are adjectives describing the noun *painting*.

Adverb A word that describes or modifies (i) a verb: *he did it gracefully* (adverb: *gracefully*), or (ii) an adjective: *a disgracefully large helping* (adverb: *disgracefully*), or (iii) another adverb: *she skated extraordinarily gracefully* (adverbs: *extraordinarily, gracefully*).

Agreement In German, adjectives agree with nouns when they stand in front of them, verbs agree with subject nouns or pronouns, pronouns agree with nouns, etc. This is a way of showing that something refers to or goes with something else. Agreement is by number (showing whether something is singular or plural), by gender (showing whether something is masculine, feminine, or neuter), and by case (showing whether something is nominative, accusative, genitive, or dative). For instance: **mit diesen grünen Socken**, *with these green socks*: **mit** must be followed by the dative, so that the noun that follows it (**die Socke**, *sock*, plural **Socken**) has to be in the dative; **dies-** adds its dative plural ending **-en** to agree with **Socken**, and so does **grün**.

Apposition Two nouns or noun phrases used together, the second one giving further information about the first: *the station master, a big man with a moustache, came in. A big man with a moustache* is in apposition to *the station master*.

Articles The little words like *a* and *the* that stand in front of nouns. In English, *the* is the definite article (it defines a particular item in a category: *the hat you've got on*); *a* or *an* is the indefinite article (it doesn't specify which item in a category: *wear a hat*, any hat).

Auxiliary Verb A verb used to help form a compound tense. In *I am walking, he has walked*, the auxiliary verbs are *to be (am)* and *to have (has)*.

Cardinal Number A number used in counting (*one, two, three, four*, etc.). Compare with Ordinal (Number).

Case Nouns, pronouns, adjectives, and articles show 'case' in German. This is an indication of the role they are playing within the sentence. There are four cases: the nominative, which is the case in which the subject of the sentence stands; the accusative, which is the case in which the direct object stands; the genitive, which shows possession; and the dative, which is the case in which the indirect object stands. The last three cases are also used after prepositions. Case still exists in English pronouns (nominative: *he*, accusative: *him*, genitive: *his*) but has almost disappeared otherwise.

Clause A self-contained section of a sentence containing a full verb: *He came in and was opening his mail when the lights went out*—'he came in', 'and (he) was opening his mail', 'when the lights went out' are clauses.

Comparative With adjectives and adverbs, the form produced (in English) by adding *-er* or prefixing '*more*': *bigger, more difficult, more easily*.

Complement The equivalent to an object with verbs such as *to be, to become*. The complement refers back to the subject and stands (correctly) in the nominative: *George became an engine driver. It is I. Engine driver* and *I* are complements.

Compound Noun Noun formed from two or more separate words, e.g. *das Dampfbügeleisen*, *steam-iron*—both English and German words are compound nouns. English often inserts a hyphen into compound nouns, especially if they are long. German does this only rarely, so some German compounds are very long indeed.

Compound Tense Tense of a verb formed by a part of that verb preceded by an auxiliary verb (*am, have, shall*, etc.): *am walking; have walked; shall walk.*

Compound Verb Verb formed by the addition of a prefix (*un-, over-, de-, dis-*, etc.) to another verb. Simple verbs: *wind, take;* compound verbs: *unwind, overtake.* German has many compound verbs. See Prefix.

Conditional Perfect Tense The tense used to express what might have happened (if something else had occurred) and formed in English with *should have (I should have walked, we should have walked)* or *would have (you would have walked, he would have walked, they would have walked).*

Conditional Tense The tense used to express what might happen (if something else occurred) and formed in English with *should (I should walk, we should walk)* or *would (you would walk, he would walk, they would walk).*

Conjugation The pattern which a type of verb follows. For instance, a regular verb in English is conjugated like this: infinitive, *to walk;* present, *I walk, he walks;* past, *he walked;* perfect, *he has walked,* etc.

Conjunction A word like *and, but, when, because* that starts a clause and joins it to the rest of the sentence.

Consonant A letter representing a sound that can only be used in conjunction with a vowel. In German, the vowels are **a, ä, e, i, o, ö, u, ü,** and (used only very occasionally) **y.** All the other letters of the alphabet are consonants.

Coordinating Conjunction A conjunction that joins two or more main clauses. Alternatively it may join two or more nouns or pronouns, or two or more phrases.

Dative The indirect object case in German. English has no dative case—we use *to* with the noun or pronoun instead. See Case.

Declension The system of endings used in German on an article, adjective, or noun to indicate case, gender, and number.

Definite Article See Articles.

Demonstrative Adjective An adjective that is used to point out a particular thing: *I'll have that cake; this cake is terrible; give me those cakes—that, this, those* are demonstrative adjectives.

Demonstrative Article Alternative name for Demonstrative Adjective.

Demonstrative Pronoun A pronoun that is used to point out a particular thing: *I'll have that; this is terrible; give me those—that, this, those* are demonstrative pronouns.

Direct Object The noun or pronoun that experiences the action of the verb: *he hits me,* direct object: *me.* See also Indirect Object.

Direct Question The simple form of the question, as put. Direct question: *Who are you?* Indirect question: *She asked me who I was. Who I was* is the indirect question. See Indirect Question.

Ending See Stem.

Feminine See Gender.

First Person See Third Person.

Future Perfect Tense The tense used to express what, at some future time, will be a past occurrence. Formed in English with *shall have* (*I shall have walked, we shall have walked*) and *will have* (*you will have walked, he will have walked, they will have walked*).

Future Tense The tense used to express a future occurrence and formed in English with *shall* (*I shall walk, we shall walk*) or *will* (*you will walk, he will walk, they will walk*).

Gender In German, a noun or pronoun may be masculine, feminine, or neuter: this is known as the gender of the noun or pronoun. The gender may correspond to the sex of the thing named, or may not. In English gender only shows in pronouns (*he, she, it,* etc.) and corresponds to the sex of the thing named. See Agreement.

Genitive One of the four cases in German: the genitive shows possession. The genitive is found in English, usually formed with *-s*: *Joan's book; his book; whose book.* See Case.

Historic Present Present tense used to relate past events, often in order to make the narrative more vivid: *So then I go into the kitchen and what do I see?*

Imperative The form of the verb that expresses a command. In English it is usually the same as the infinitive without *to*: infinitive, *to walk*, imperative, *walk!*

Imperfect Subjunctive In German, alternative name for the Past Subjunctive. See Subjunctive.

Imperfect Tense In German, alternative name for the Past Tense. See Past Tense.

Impersonal Verb A verb whose subject is an unspecific *it* or *there*: *it is raining; there's no need for that.*

Indefinite Adjective An adjective such as *each, such, some, other, every, several* that does not specify identifiable people or objects.

Indefinite Article See Articles.

Indefinite Pronoun A pronoun such as *somebody, anybody, something, anything, everybody, nobody* that does not specify identifiable people or objects.

Indirect Object The noun or pronoun at which the direct object is aimed. In English it either has or can have *to* in front of it: *I passed it (to) him*, indirect object *(to) him*; *I gave her my address (I gave my address to her)*, indirect object *(to) her*. In these examples *it* and *my address* are direct objects. In German as in English some verbs take an indirect object only.

Indirect Question A question (without a question mark) in a subordinate clause. It is introduced by some such expression as *I wonder if . . .* , *do you know where . . .* , *I'll tell him when . . .* , *he's asking who . . .* Direct question: *When is he coming?* Indirect question: *I don't know when he's coming.*

Infinitive The basic part of the verb from which other parts are derived. In English, it is normally preceded by *to*: *to walk, to run*.

Inseparable Prefix See Prefix.

Inseparable Verb A compound verb consisting of a simple verb with an inseparable prefix. See Prefix.

Interrogative The question form of the verb.

Interrogative Adjective A question word (in English *which . . .?* or *what . . .?*) used adjectivally with a following noun: *which book do you mean?*

Interrogative Adverb An adverb that introduces a direct question, in English *why?*, *when?*, *how?*, etc. In indirect questions the same words function as conjunctions, joining the question to the main clause. *Why do you say that?*—direct question, *why* is an interrogative adverb; *I don't know why you say that*—indirect question, *why* is a conjunction.

Interrogative Pronoun A pronoun that asks a question, in English *who?* and *what?*

Intransitive Of verbs: having no direct object.

Irregular Verb In German, a verb that does not follow the standard pattern of a regular (also called a 'weak') verb. See Strong Verb; Mixed Verb.

Main Clause A clause within a sentence that could stand on its own and still make sense. For example: *He came in when he* *was ready. He came in* is a main clause (it makes sense standing on its own); *when he was ready* is a subordinate clause (it can't stand on its own and still make sense).

Masculine See Gender.

Mixed Verb In German, a verb that both changes its vowel in the past (like a strong verb) and also adds characteristic endings (like a weak verb). See Strong Verb; Weak Verb.

Modal Verbs (literally 'verbs of mood'). These are the auxiliary verbs (other than *have* and *be*) that always appear with a dependent infinitive: *I can walk, I must walk, I will walk—can, must, will* are modal verbs.

Neuter See Gender.

Nominative One of the four cases in German. The nominative is the case the subject of the sentence stands in. See Case.

Noun A word that names a person or thing. *Peter, box, glory, indecision* are nouns.

Noun Clause A clause that is the equivalent of a noun within the sentence: *I don't want to catch whatever you've got* (*whatever you've got* is a clause for which we might substitute a noun, e.g. *measles*).

Number With nouns, pronouns, etc.—the state of being either singular or plural. See Agreement.

Object See Direct Object; Indirect Object.

Ordinal (Number) A number such as *first, second, third, fourth*, normally used adjectivally referring to one thing in a series.

Passive The basic tenses of a verb are active. Passive tenses are the set of tenses that are used in order to make the person or thing experiencing the action of the verb (normally the object) into the subject of the verb. Active (basic tense): *I discover it*, passive: *it is discovered (by me)*; active: *he ate them*, passive: *they were eaten (by him)*.

Passive Infinitive The passive form of the infinitive, where the implied subject suffers the action of the verb. In English: active infinitive, *to eat*; passive infinitive, *to be eaten*. The perfect infinitive can also be put into the passive: perfect infinitive, active: *to have eaten*; perfect infinitive, passive, *to have been eaten*.

Past Continuous, Perfect Continuous In English, the past tenses formed using -*ing*, implying that something was or has been continuing to occur: past continuous: *I was walking*, perfect continuous: *I have been walking*.

Past Participle The part of the verb used to form compound past tenses. In English, it usually ends in -*ed*. Verb: *to walk*; past participle: *walked*; perfect tense: *I have walked*.

Past Tense In German, the tense used in written narrative and, for some verbs, in speech as well; often the equivalent to the English past tense: **ich machte**, *I made*.

Perfect Continuous See Past Continuous.

Perfect Infinitive The past form of the infinitive, formed in English from *to have* + past participle: *to have walked*.

Perfect Tense The past tense that, in English, is formed by using *have* + past participle: *I have walked*. The German perfect is usually formed in the same way (**haben** + past participle), but its use is not quite the same.

Personal Pronouns Subject and object pronouns referring to people or things (*he, him, she, her, it*, etc.).

Phrasal Verb In English, a verb made by combining a simple verb with a preposition or adverb: *run out, jump up, stand down*. English phrasal verbs often correspond to German separable verbs. See Separable Verbs.

Phrase A self-contained section of a sentence that does not contain a full verb. *Being late as usual, he arrived at a quarter past eleven*: *at a quarter past eleven* is a phrase; present and past participles are not full verbs, so *being late as usual* is also a phrase. Compare Clause.

Pluperfect Continuous In English, the equivalent tense to the pluperfect using *had been* + *-ing*, implying that something had been going on (when something else happened), e.g.: *I had been walking for an hour, when . . .*

Pluperfect Tense The past tense that, in English, is formed by using *had* + past participle: *I had walked*. The German pluperfect is usually formed and used in the same way (with the past tense of *haben* + past participle).

Possessive Adjective An adjective that indicates possession; in English, *my, your, her*, etc.: *that is my book*.

Possessive Article Alternative name for Possessive Adjective.

Possessive Pronoun A pronoun that indicates possession; in English, *mine, yours, hers*, etc.: *that book is mine*.

Prefix In German, a short addition to the beginning of a verb. This may form an integral part of the verb (it is then called an inseparable prefix and the verb an inseparable verb), or it may in certain circumstances separate off (it is then a separable prefix and the verb a separable verb). German separable verbs quite often correspond to English phrasal verbs: **aufstehen**, *to stand up*; **ich stehe auf**, *I stand up*.

Preposition A word like *in, over, near, across* that stands in front of a noun or pronoun relating it to the rest of the sentence.

Present Continuous See Present Tense.

Present Participle The part of the verb that in English ends in *-ing*: *to walk*: present participle, *walking*.

Present Tense The tense of the verb that refers to things now happening regularly (simple present: *I walk*), or happening at the moment (present continuous: *I am walking*).

Pronoun A word such as *he, she, which, mine* that stands instead of a noun (usually already mentioned).

Question See Direct Question; Indirect Question.

Reciprocal Pronoun A pronoun like *each other*, *one another* which implies that one inflicts the verb's action on the other member of a plural subject and not on oneself. *They shot themselves* is a reflexive verb; *they shot each other* is a reciprocal verb.

Reflexive Pronoun See Reflexive Verb.

Reflexive Verb A verb whose object is the same as its subject: *he likes himself*, *she can dress herself*. *Himself, herself* are reflexive pronouns.

Relative Pronoun A pronoun that introduces a subordinate clause and at the same time allows that clause to function as an adjective or noun. In English the relative pronouns are *who(m), which, whose, that,* and *what. Tell me what you know!*: *what you know* is a noun clause and the direct object of *tell me*. It is introduced by the relative pronoun *what. That's the lad who stole my wallet*: *who stole my wallet* is an adjectival clause describing *lad*. It is introduced by the relative pronoun *who*.

Second Person See Third Person.

Separable Prefix See Prefix.

Separable Verb A verb formed from a simple verb and a separable prefix. See Prefix.

Simple Tense A one-word tense of a verb: *I walk, I run* (as opposed to a compound tense: *I am walking, I was running*).

Stem The part of a verb to which endings indicating tense, person, etc. are added. Verb: *to walk*: stem, *walk-*: *he walk-s, he walk-ed*, etc.

Strong Verb In German, an irregular verb, showing its past tense by a vowel change.

Subject (of verb, clause, or sentence) The noun or pronoun that initiates the action of the verb: *George walked*, subject: *George*; *he hit George*, subject: *he*.

Subjunctive In German, a set of tenses that express doubt or unlikelihood. The subjunctive still exists in only a few expressions in English: *If I were you* [but I'm not], *I'd go now* (*I were* is subjunctive—the normal past tense is *I was*).

Subordinate Clause A clause in a sentence that depends, in order to make sense, on a main clause. See Main Clause.

Subordinating Conjunction A conjunction that introduces a subordinate clause.

Superlative With adjectives and adverbs, the form produced by adding *-est* or prefixing 'most': *biggest, most difficult, most easily*.

Tense The form of a verb that indicates when the action takes place (e.g. present tense: *I walk*; past tense: *I walked*).

Third Person *He, she, it, they* (and their derivatives, like *him, his, her, their*), or any noun, or any indefinite or demonstrative pronoun. The first person is *I* or *we* (and their derivatives), the second person is *you* (and its derivatives).

Transitive Of verbs: having a direct object.

Umlaut The only accent used in German: the two dots ('diaeresis') placed over the vowels **a, o, u**, to indicate a change in the way they are pronounced.

Verb The word that tells you what the subject of the clause does: *he goes; she dislikes me; have you eaten it?; they know nothing*—*goes, dislikes, have eaten, know* are verbs.

Verbal Noun Part of the verb (in English, usually the present participle) used as a noun: *smoking is bad for you*: verbal noun, *smoking*.

Vowel A letter representing a sound that can be pronounced by itself without the addition of other sounds. In German, the vowels are **a, ä, e, i, o, ö, u, ü,** and (used only very occasionally) **y**.

Weak Verb The name given to a regular verb in German—one that follows the standard verb pattern.

Index

English prepositions should be looked up in the alphabetical list on page 188.

Irregular verbs should be looked up in the alphabetical list on page 73.

Verb constructions (preposition, case) should be looked up in the alphabetical list of verbs on page 53.

Definitions of grammatical terms will be found in the glossary on page 251.